THE
TORTURE DOCTOR

H. H. HOLMES,
The Arch Fiend. After a late photograph.

THE
TORTURE DOCTOR

DAVID FRANKE

HAWTHORN BOOKS, INC.
PUBLISHERS/NEW YORK

For Holly,
with love

THE TORTURE DOCTOR

Copyright © 1975 by David Franke. Copyright under International and Pan-American Copyright Conventions. All rights reserved, including the right to reproduce this book or portions thereof in any form, except for the inclusion of brief quotations in a review. All inquiries should be addressed to Hawthorn Books, Inc., 260 Madison Avenue, New York, New York 10016. This book was manufactured in the United States of America and published simultaneously in Canada by Prentice-Hall of Canada, Limited, 1870 Birchmount Road, Scarborough, Ontario.

Library of Congress Catalog Card Number: 75-2561
ISBN: 0-8015-7832-9

1 2 3 4 5 6 7 8 9 10

But that I am forbid
To tell the secrets of my prison-house,
I could a tale unfold whose lightest word
Would harrow up thy soul, freeze thy young blood,
Make thy two eyes, like stars, start from their spheres,
Thy knotted and combined locks to part,
And each particular hair to stand on end,
Like quills upon the fretful porcupine.

*   *   *

Foul deeds will rise,
Though all the earth o'erwhelm them,
     to men's eyes.

—*Hamlet*

Great criminals, as original characters,
stand forward on the canvas of humanity
as worthy objects of our especial study.

—Edmund Burke

CONTENTS

3

CONSTERNATION IN CHICAGO 33

H. H. Holmes, the Alleged Insurance Swindler, Well Known in This City. FINDS EASY PREY. Swindled With Dash and Vim and Had Victims Untold. READS LIKE ROMANCE. Begins His Chicago Career by Building a "Castle" With Other People's Money. FOND OF THE SOCIETY OF WOMEN.

4

A NEW CONFESSION FROM HOLMES 49

Says Pitezel a Suicide; the Children in London with M. Williams, His Former Typewriter. ANOTHER FABRICATION? Police Put Detective Geyer on Trail of Children. HE FACES GREAT ODDS.

5

CHILDREN'S BLOOD SHED 59

Bodies of Two Pitezel Girls Discovered in Toronto Cellar. SAD SCENE IN MORGUE. Mrs. Pitezel Identifies the Corpses of Her Children. HOWARD PITEZEL'S FATE JUST AS TRAGIC. His Bones Found in the Chimney of a Cottage Near Indianapolis. HOLMES SILENT.

6

HOLMES CASTLE REVEALS HORRORS 83

Queer Tank Discovered, Along with Vats of Quicklime, Skeletons, and Charred Bones; Proof that Bodies were Cremated in Englewood. FOUL GAS TAKES FIRE. Explosion Disturbs the Searchers in the Castle's Basement. MORE CRIMES ADDED. Common Fates Awaited Mrs. Conner and Daughter, Miss Emeline Cigrand, and Williams Sisters. HOW MANY VICTIMS?

FOREWORD

In the early 1890s the citizens of Chicago began to realize that they were living in a great city which was a fitting place for the World's Columbian Exposition of 1893. They had sent a committee to Washington to bid for the show, familiarly called the world's fair, and it took a few months, after Congress gave approval, for the idea to dawn that Chicago *was* the best site in the country for an exposition which the entire world would attend. It wasn't merely the central location, where the transcontinental railroads came together—there was something in the air out on Lake Michigan that seemed to promise whatever it was you wanted the future to bring, and the sky over the lake seemed the only limit to American plans for perfecting this country and reorganizing the world on humane and rational lines. The historian Henry Adams, who found the fair a fascinating study, wrote that, to understand the spirit of the age, "one must begin in Chicago."

Visitors found what Rudyard Kipling had identified as "a real city." There were huge buildings in the downtown Loop, resting their incalculable tonnage on subterranean platforms of cement and steel that the engineers called rafts, giving laymen a startling suggestion that the structures were floating on a swamp. On the North, West, and South sides one could find smaller editions of the Loop, business centers of populous neighborhoods with every type of shop and service available to people who crowded the sidewalks of long streets running west from the lake. These neighborhood business districts with their offices, hotels, theaters, and apartment houses were signs of true metropolitan life. They indicated a city in which one might disappear, if one wished to, by moving from Wilson Avenue on the North Side, for example, to Ashland Avenue on the West Side, or to Hyde Park on the South Side, or to Englewood, another thriving enclave down that way, which centered on Sixty-third Street.

Young men and women flocked to Chicago from Indiana, Michigan, Wisconsin, and downstate Illinois, drawn by the possibility of starting careers free from the constant observation of the small towns. The city's indifference was exactly what they needed, for it encouraged them to find themselves as they really were. We can list successful seekers by the score; here are just a few. There were George Ade; Edgar Lee Masters; Clarence Darrow; Frances Willard, who founded the Women's Christian Temperance Union; Vachel Lindsay; the first Marshall Field; Potter Palmer, whose wife used her position as society queen to help women everywhere; Aaron Montgomery Ward, who founded the mail-order firm and saved the lakefront for the people of Chicago; John Wellborn Root, who designed the Monadnock Building and died too young; and Jane Addams, the pioneer social worker who may without exaggeration be listed as a saint. All these and more came into the bracing and stimulating air of late nineteenth-century Chicago and reacted to it by expressing themselves in ways for which we should still be grateful. Yes, that also goes for Marshall Field; the frosty merchant prince never forgot his obligation to give value, and instructed his staff, "The customer is always right."

There were those in the city, however, whose only interest in the customer was robbery, sometimes accompanied by mayhem. During and after the Civil War, Chicago attracted blacklegs, thieves, swindlers, and hoodlums by the thousand, accompanied by an army of bawds and rum sellers who colonized many neighborhoods and established the traditions of Chicago crime which have furnished material for thousands of articles and hundreds of books. And yet, up to the present, there has been no authoritative work on the subject of the book to which this is foreword—no reliable documented biography of a man named Herman W. Mudgett, a.k.a. Henry H. Holmes. He was an industrious killer of harmless human beings. Most of his crimes took place in Chicago.

The *Guiness Book of World Records* lists him as "the most prolific murderer known in recent criminal history."

Mudgett-Holmes used the freedom and lack of neighborhood surveillance in metropolitan Chicago for activities which would seem incredible were it not for David Franke's painstaking research into the facts which lie beneath the legends that have collected around "the Monster of Sixty-third Street." For it was on that street, in Englewood, that this man engaged in certain dreadful enterprises which caused an unknown number of native Chicagoans, together with visitors to the fair, to disappear—and not to another part of town for a few months, but to a place we know not of, and forever. What are we to make of this monster? Why did we not get from this Chicagoan the plans of a Root, the verses of a Masters, or even something to compare with the kindness of Jane Addams? Good influences in plenty were there, but Mudgett-Holmes received his instructions, it would seem, from a sinister source. And it has remained for Mr. Franke, whose research is impeccable, and whose writing is a delight, to sum up the story and follow the monster to the gallows. It is a story of primal fascination, and as I think of it, I realize that it is now past time for the writer of this foreword, like the late Ed Sullivan at CBS, to get himself off and let the show go on.

FINIS FARR

ACKNOWLEDGMENTS

I am indebted to many friends and associates for their assistance and encouragement while I was writing this book. First mention should go to Finis Farr, to whom I am indebted for introducing me to H. H. Holmes in his delightful *Chicago: A Personal History of America's Most American City*, and later for his enthusiasm and kind consent to write the foreword. I am particularly indebted to Robert Ritchie, for his research assistance in Philadelphia, and to the Honorable John Conlan, George Archibald, and Sue Brands in Washington, D.C. I also gratefully acknowledge the aid and encouragement of Durwood and Rita Franke, Donald Lambro, Phillip Lambro, Katherine Williams, Frank Carrington, and Richard J. Brzeczek, executive assistant to the superintendent of police in Chicago. I am indebted to my colleague in editorial crime, Martin A. Gross, for suggesting the title, and to Jameson and Caroline Campaigne, Jr., for their hospitality and for providing me with a midnight tour of presentday Englewood.

This book could not have been completed without the expert assistance of the staffs of the libraries I used throughout my research, namely, the Library of Congress in Washington; the library of the Chicago Historical Society, the Chicago Public Library, and the Newberry Library in Chicago; the Philadelphia Free Library and the Biddle Law Library in that same city; the New

York Public Library; Sterling Memorial Library at Yale University; and the Archives Division of the Texas State Library in Austin. Thanks are due in particular to Mr. Joseph C. Lutz of the history and travel department of the Chicago Public Library, and Mr. Neal J. Ney, assistant reference librarian at the Chicago Historical Society.

Above all, I am grateful to my wife, Holly, who in addition to the travails of pregnancy and the birth of our first child, Melissa, had to contend with the much more troublesome birth of this volume; to my father- and mother-in-law, Mr. and Mrs. Pascal Lambro, for rearranging their schedules to make it possible for me to travel and continue my research during this hectic period; to Melissa, for her cooperation in causing as little disruption as possible; and to my agent, Henriette Neatrour, and my editor at Hawthorn Books, Elizabeth Backman, for their kind consideration of the havoc even a perfect infant can inflict on an author's deadlines and good intentions.

* * *

Considering the sensational nature of Holmes' career, and the tremendous impact of his exposure and trial in the 1890s, it is surprising how little literature is available on this character who, to my mind, certainly qualifies as America's foremost criminal. Even so, more than enough is available to fill a volume many times the size of this one.

In the matter of the murder of Benjamin F. Pitezel, and related events, I relied primarily on the transcript of Holmes' trial, where witnesses were under oath. This was published as *The Trial of Herman W. Mudgett* (Philadelphia: George T. Bisel, 1897). It is not available from the Library of Congress, and the only copies of which I am aware are in the Philadelphia Free Library and the Biddle Law Library.

For the story of the murder of the Pitezel children, and Holmes' flight throughout the Northeast and Canada with Mrs. Pitezel and Miss Yoke, I placed primary emphasis on the account of Detective Frank P. Geyer, *The Holmes-Pitezel Case* (Philadelphia:

Publishers' Union, 1896). It is available at the Library of Congress, the New York Public Library, and the library of the Chicago Historical Society.

Any statement from Holmes must be taken with a heavy dose of skepticism, but it is nevertheless fascinating to read *Holmes' Own Story* (Philadelphia: Burk & McFetridge Co., 1895), which includes his Moyamensing Prison diary. It will be found in the rare books room of the Library of Congress.

Of lesser value among the books published in the 1890s are: Robert L. Corbitt, *The Holmes Castle* (Chicago: Corbitt & Morrison, 1895), available at the library of the Chicago Historical Society and on microfilm at the Library of Congress; *Holmes, The Arch Fiend, or: A Carnival of Crime* (Cincinnati: Barclay & Co., 189-), available at the Library of Congress and the New York Public Library; *Sold to Satan, Holmes—A poor wife's sad story, not a mere rehash, but something new never before published. A living victim* (Philadelphia: Old Franklin Publishing House, ca. 1896), which I found only in the rare books room of the Library of Congress. The latter is also available at the Library of Congress in a German-language edition, under the title *Dem Teufel verkauft Holmes! Traurige Geschichte einer armen Frau. Ein lebendes Opfer.* And in the Swedish language the Library of Congress has Lars A. Stenholt, *Massemorderen Holmes, alias Mudgett, En historisk berettelse om denne store Jorbryders misgjarninger* (Minneapolis: W. Kriedt Publishing Co., 1896).

Of more recent vintage, in book form, there is only a Gold Medal Books paperback by Charles Boswell and Lewis Thompson, *The Girls in Nightmare House* (New York: Fawcett Publications, 1955), and a novel based on Holmes' life by Robert Bloch, *American Gothic* (New York: Simon & Schuster, 1974).

Holmes has been given his due in various histories of Chicago and of American crime, of which the most enjoyable accounts are in Finis Farr, *Chicago: A Personal History of America's Most American City* (New Rochelle, N.Y.: Arlington House, 1973), and Herbert Asbury, *Gem of the Prairie: An Informal History of the Chicago Underworld* (New York: Alfred A. Knopf, 1940). The dedicated Holmesophile will also find summaries of his career in a number of other books, and among the ones I consulted were: Jay Robert Nash, *Bloodletters and Badmen* (New York: M. Evans, 1973); Allen Churchill, *A Pictorial History of American Crime, 1849–1929* (New York: Holt, Rinehart & Winston, 1964); Sewell Peaslee Wright, ed., *Chicago Murders* (New York: Duell, Sloan and Pearce, 1945); H. B. Irving, *A Book of Remarkable Criminals* (Westport, Conn.: Hyperion Press, 1974; reprint of ed. published by George H. Doran Co., New York, 1918); James D. Horan and Howard Swiggett, *The Pinkerton Story* (New York: G. P. Putnam's Sons, 1951); Matthew W. Pinkerton, *Murder in All Ages* (Chicago: A. E. Pinkerton and Co., 1898).

H. H. Holmes was, above all, good newspaper copy, and I had to rely on newspapers as my primary source for accounts of his Chicago swindling career, the Castle, the emotions surrounding his trial (the cold type of the transcript tells but half of the story), his final confession, and his execution. The reader is advised, therefore, to read these portions of the story more for enjoyment than for any literal truth; the interpretive reporting of the 1890s makes today's journalists look like Boy Scouts, and one often wonders if different witnesses to the same event were truly inhabiting the same planet. Among the newspapers I consulted were, in Chicago, the *Inter Ocean, Herald, Times-Herald, Tribune*, and *Daily News;* in Philadelphia, the *Public Ledger* and the *Inquirer;* and in New York, the *Times, World*, and *Herald.*

The Chicago police department, unfortunately, maintains no files prior to 1929.

Of particular value in my study of Holmes' Englewood were Gerald E. Sullivan, ed., *The Story of Englewood, 1835–1923* (Chicago: Foster & McDonnell, 1924); *The Town of Lake Directory* for the years 1886, 1887, 1888, and 1889 (Chicago: R. R. Donnelley & Sons); and *The Englewood Directory 1890* (Chicago: Geo. Amberg & Co.). Also consulted were the maps in the archives of the Chicago Historical Society; the Englewood Golden Jubilee Edition (November 10, 1940) of the *Southtown Economist*, a neighborhood newspaper; and the following: J. H. Brayton, compiler, *Englewood Directory for 1882* (Englewood, Ill.: Tousley, Denison & Tousley); *Financial & Commercial Chicago*

ACKNOWLEDGMENTS

With Environs Illustrated, 1804-1891 (Philadelphia: Belgravia Publishing Co., 1891); Harold M. Mayer and Richard C. Wade, *Chicago: Growth of a Metropolis* (Chicago: University of Chicago Press, 1969); John J. Flinn, *The Standard Guide to Chicago for the Year 1891*, also listed as *Chicago: The Marvelous City of the West* (Chicago: Flinn & Sheppard, 1890); George E. Moran, compiler, *Moran's Dictionary of Chicago and Its Vicinity* (Chicago, 1893).

DAVID FRANKE
Ridgefield, Connecticut
August 1975

HERMAN WEBSTER MUDGETT
alias H. H. HOLMES

Alias Henry Howard Holmes
Alias H. M. (Henry Mansfield) Howard
Alias D. T. Pratt
Alias Harry (Henry) Gordon
Alias Edward Hatch
Alias J. A. Judson
Alias Alexander E. Cook
Alias A. C. Hayes
Alias George H. Howell
Alias G. D. Hale
Alias Mr. Hall

BENJAMIN FULLER PITEZEL
(B. F. Pitezel)

Alias B. F. Perry
Alias Benton T. Lyman
Alias L. T. Benton
Alias H. S. Campbell
Alias Robert Jones
Alias Robert E. Phelps

THE
TORTURE DOCTOR

1
A BODY IS FOUND
IN PHILADELPHIA

B. F. Perry, Dealer in Patents,
Apparently Victim of Explosion.

IS PERRY REALLY PITEZEL?

Widow, in St. Louis, Sends
Lawyer and Daughter to
Identify Body, Claim Insurance.

GRISLY SCENE
AT POTTER'S FIELD

Fidelity Mutual Insurance,
a Philadelphia Firm,
Agrees Body is B. F. Pitezel.

$10,000 POLICY PAID PROMPTLY;
A GENEROUS GESTURE

Eugene Smith was a carpenter by trade, but work had been scarce for some years and he had plenty of time to devote to his dream of becoming a successful and prosperous inventor. That dream was more than idle speculation, for despite his lack of any advanced education, Smith was handy in practical matters and had devised a saw set that could sharpen a dull saw with a minimum of physical effort. Certainly there must be a market for such a useful device, he thought, but how could he, a laborer of limited contacts, exploit that need? What should he do first? How could he go about finding an investor or manufacturer who had the capital and resources to put the set on the market?

Smith became interested at once, therefore, when a neighbor told him of a shop on Callowhill Street with a sign in the window advertising a trade in patents. Perhaps here was the expert assistance he needed. Early the next morning, a Thursday, the twenty-second of August, 1894, Smith walked over to Callowhill Street. This was not the most fashionable neighborhood in town, for across the street was the old abandoned station of the Philadelphia and Reading Railroad, but it was with some excitement that Smith noticed the muslin sheet stretched across the window at number 1316, on which was printed in crude black and red letters, "B. F. Perry, Patents Bought and Sold." The house was one of a row of similar red brick residences, each two and a half stories high. The first floor, with its oversized store window, had apparently been converted into a place of business. Iron stanchions rose from the brick sidewalk in front of the house, but they stood bare and ugly in the sun without the benefit of the canvas awnings intended for them.

The carpenter walked up two steps, opened the door, and found himself in a sparsely furnished office. He introduced himself to Perry, a man nearly six feet tall, with dark brown hair, a thin moustache, and the beginnings of a goatee. A visitor of greater refinement might have been skeptical of the business potential of this Perry, for despite a good physical frame and the neat dress of a white-collar worker, his narrow, sharp countenance and irregular teeth made him look old for his age, his calloused hands divulged a history of manual labor, and his breath often smelled strongly of whiskey. But Smith was not of a mind or temperament to be critical, and he told Perry of his hopes for his invention. It sounded like a good thing, Perry replied, and he thought he could place it.

Flushed with anticipation, Smith worked on the model of his invention and returned the following Monday to place it in Perry's custody. He paid another visit on Thursday, each time talking with Perry for fifteen or twenty minutes. It was during the Monday visit, after he delivered the model of the saw set to Perry and got a receipt, that he made an observation, the significance of which he could not have been even faintly aware of at the time. A man walked in as they were talking, turned quickly to give a nod to Perry, and continued upstairs. Perry excused himself to his client, saying he would be back in a few minutes, and he followed the man up the stairway. A moment later Perry returned. "Well, my business is done with you," Smith said, preparing to leave. "There's no use in my detaining you any longer." The unannounced caller was still upstairs when he left.

By Monday, September 3, Smith was anxious to see if any progress had been made in the placement of his invention. When he arrived at 1316 Callowhill that afternoon, he found the door closed but not locked, so he walked in. No one was around, and he called, "Mr. Perry," at the top of his voice. No answer. Smith sat in a chair and waited for fifteen minutes. He thought that something seemed odd—things were scattered about, and everything was not as neat or in place as it was when he had visited there before. At the back of the office he noticed Perry's hat and cuffs hanging on a nail in the hall, but there was no evidence of the patent man himself. Then a man dressed in black, and carrying a black bag, came in from the street and asked where the boss was. "I don't know," Smith replied. "I'm waiting for him myself. Please take a seat, and I will see if I can find him anywhere." But the man wouldn't take a seat, so they both left, Smith closing the door as he left.

Perhaps he was worried about the safety of his model in an unattended office; at any rate, Smith returned promptly the next morning at nine o'clock. Again he found the door closed but unlocked. Again he found everything in the room just as he had left it. Again he noticed the hat and cuffs hanging in the same place, and again he cried out, "Mr. Perry," at the top of his voice, and received no answer. He took a seat, but he began to worry. "There must be something wrong," he said to himself, "when he leaves his place open."

Smith got up and walked up the stairs at the back of the hall. Reaching the second-floor landing, he faced the bedroom, noticing a bed with bedclothes on it but no Perry. He turned to his left, and through a door that opened to the back room he saw a sight that stopped him frozen in horror—a body, apparently lifeless, lying prostrate on the floor. Smith didn't stop to inspect the body or the scene but ran out of the house and to the nearest police station on Buttonwood Street. Two officers heeded his call for help and on the way back to Callowhill Street picked up Dr. William J. Scott.

A terrible stench stopped them short when they entered the back room—putrefaction had set in, and the upper part of the body was especially decomposed. The body was lying in a very peaceful position on its back, the right arm bent at the elbow and resting on the chest, the left arm at its side. The window was slightly raised and the shutters opened, allowing the sun to strike the body nearly all day long, which explained its extensive decomposition where it was not protected by clothing. Dr. Scott found the face especially discolored and distorted, and he recalled later that "his tongue was swollen and stuck out of his mouth, and red fluid issued from his mouth. Any little pressure on the stomach or over the chest would cause this fluid to flow more rapidly, and to raise the head a little would cause it to flow more rapidly. His mustache was singed, just as though a flame had flashed over and singed it a little bit, and also the eyebrow and the side of his head or hair." The corpse's right breast and outer portion of the arm were similarly burned. "At his head was laid a pipe recently filled, and it looked very much as if he had taken a match and made a puff from it."

It was these indications of burning that led to speculation there had been an explosion. A cracked and broken bottle lay on the floor, and shelves contained a number of uncorked bottles filled with a red-colored fluid that apparently was a mixture of benzine (which is explosive), chloroform, and a touch of ammonia. Next to the corpse's head was a burned match, and it was established that the tobacco in the pipe had been lit.

Conveniently enough, the city morgue was directly to the rear of 1316 Callowhill Street, and that same day the body was removed to the morgue and an autopsy performed by Dr. William K. Mattern, one of the coroner's physicians. Dr. Scott had become interested in the case and so he was present, too. They reported it as a well-nourished body of between 170 and 180 pounds, heavy and muscular. The brain, heart, and liver were normal, though his kidneys were what are called "pig-back" kidneys, peculiar to people who are alcoholic. The heart was empty and the lungs congested, indicating sudden death, and the stomach was empty of food but contained a fluid found to be chloroform. While the police leaned to an explosion as the cause of death, the physicians thought it to be chloroform poisoning. Whatever the cause, it had resulted in paralysis of the involuntary muscles, as the bladder had emptied and regurgitation had taken place from the mouth where the body lay.

Because of the extensive decomposition and burns, it was difficult to identify the body with certainty, but the clothing was the same as Eugene Smith had seen Perry wear, and the general appearance matched Perry's. The coroner's jury officially found the body to be that of B. F. Perry, but then the question remained— who was Perry? And had his death been accidental, a suicide, or murder? Nobody particularly cared to find answers to those questions, it seemed. The Philadelphia newspapers ran short stories on the death, which were picked up by the wire services, but since nobody came forth to identify and claim the body, B. F. Perry, whoever he was, was quietly buried in Potter's Field.

* * *

Even as the unclaimed body was lying in the city morgue, the Fidelity Mutual Life Insurance Company of Philadelphia received a telegram from its St. Louis manager, George B. Stadden, carrying the startling news that "B. F. Perry, found dead in Philadelphia, is claimed to be B. F. Pitezel, who is insured on 044145. Investigate before remains leave there."

This was followed by a letter to the insurance company from Jeptha D. Howe, a St. Louis attorney, stating that he repre-

BENJAMIN F. PITEZEL

sented Mrs. Carrie A. Pitezel, the wife of Benjamin F. Pitezel and beneficiary of a $10,000 policy he held with Fidelity Mutual. Howe added that he would visit Philadelphia soon with a member of the Pitezel family for the purpose of identifying the Perry body as Pitezel and claiming the insurance money.

A search through the company's books disclosed that they had indeed insured Pitezel for that amount on November 9, 1893. Policy No. 044145 had been taken out through the firm's Chicago branch office, so instructions were forwarded at once to Edward H. Cass, cashier at the Chicago branch, asking him to find out all he could about Pitezel and to contact any persons who knew him. Insurance companies tend to become suspicious when policy-holders die within a year of taking out a large policy—and we must remember that 10,000 gold-backed 1894 dollars were the equivalent of at least $60,000 in today's inflated greenbacks. Suspicions grow rapidly when—as in this case—the most recent semiannual premium of $157.50 had been received by telegraphic money order on the last day of grace, August 9, 1894.

Cass had received that premium payment, but he had not written the policy so he contacted the agent who had. The agent knew of only one person familiar with B. F. Pitezel—an H. H. Holmes of Wilmette, Illinois. Cass checked with the home office and they told him to contact Holmes, which he proceeded to do.

9

When Cass arrived at the Holmeses' comfortable but unpretentious home, he was met by a most attractive lady in her early thirties who introduced herself as Mrs. Myrta Holmes. Her husband was away on business, she said, but she would forward any message from Mr. Cass since they were continually in touch. She would not give him a current address where he could reach Holmes directly, so Cass handed her a letter and a clipping from a Chicago paper which stated erroneously that Pitezel had been found in Chicago, and asked her to send it to her husband.

On September 18, Cass received a reply from Holmes postmarked Columbus, Ohio. Holmes stated that he did not know who did Pitezel's dental work—one of Cass' inquiries—"though I do not think he took very good care of his teeth and may have had none done. I remember that seven or eight years ago when working for me, he had to give up work for some time on account of neuralgia in his teeth."

Holmes gave a general description of Pitezel and added that "he also had some sort of a warty growth on the back or side of his neck, which prevented him from wearing a collar when working. Aside from these points, I can think of nothing to distinguish him from other men, unless it be that his forehead was lower than the average and crown of head higher, causing one to notice same.

"If the identity is not cleared up by the time you receive this letter and you wish me to," Holmes added, "I will go to Chicago any time after Wednesday next, provided you will pay my transportation there and return. . . . I would be willing to go without pay in ordinary times, but can hardly afford to do so now."

Holmes must have been in dire financial need for he did not let the matter rest, but continued by claiming that "Mr. Pitezel is owing me One hundred and eighty dollars, and if he is in reality dead, I should be glad to have that amount retained from the sum payable on his policy and apply same on my own, as I very much need it. . . . My affairs are not in a good condition and I need insurance more than at any time. I have done a good deal for his family within the past eight years and I think if need be, I could get an order from his wife, authorizing you to retain the amount due me."

The following day Cass received another letter from Holmes,

this time from Cincinnati. "Since writing to you yesterday," he said, "I have seen from a file of Philadelphia papers, that the supposed body of Pitezel is in the hands of the coroner there instead of in Chicago, as per clipping you sent me. I shall be in Baltimore in a day or two, and I will take an afternoon train to Philadelphia and call on your office there, and if they wish me to do so, I will go with some representative of theirs to the coroner's, and I think I can tell if the man there is Pitezel; from what I read here, I cannot see anything to lead me to think that the person killed was other than a man by the name of Perry."

Cass thanked Holmes for the information and assured him that his expenses to and from Baltimore would be defrayed if he would come to Philadelphia to identify the corpse.

Holmes lost no time in getting to Philadelphia. On September 20 he arrived at the Fidelity building and talked with L. G. Fouse, the company's president. A man of slight build, medium in height, and weighing barely 150 pounds, Holmes nevertheless had an erect and manly bearing. At 34 years of age his brown hair was not too sparse, and a well-kept moustache shaded his small mouth. Women found him attractive, for he dressed immaculately, his large blue eyes were mild and gentle, his voice soft and low. Besides, he was well educated. While not necessarily effeminate, it was easy to consider that he was what is called a "lady's man." A more physical man might have called him "pretty" in mild deprecation.

Holmes asked Fouse about the circumstances of the death and the reported cause of death and remarked that it was a peculiar case. He, in turn, was asked for a description of Pitezel, which he gave.

Mr. Fouse told Holmes that Mrs. Pitezel's attorney, Jeptha D. Howe, would be arriving shortly with a member of the family, and that the body would probably be exhumed from Potter's Field. He suggested that Holmes leave his Philadelphia address so they could contact him and obtain his opinion of the identity of the body. Holmes replied that he had business in Nicetown, a suburb of Philadelphia, and that if he went away the next day he would leave word where he could be reached. Otherwise, he would call again at the office the next morning.

Jeptha D. Howe did arrive the following day and produced a

11

letter of attorney from Mrs. Pitezel and a number of letters she had received from her husband while he was living as B. F. Perry at 1316 Callowhill Street. Howe said that Pitezel had run into financial difficulties in Tennessee, which is why he had changed his name and location, but he provided few details about the nature of those troubles. Mr. Fouse told the attorney that the company was convinced that Perry and Pitezel were indeed the same person, but they were not convinced that the dead man found was Pitezel, the man they had insured. Howe was astonished. President Fouse asked him to give a description of Pitezel, and the description agreed in all respects with that of the dead man.

Pitezel's second oldest daughter, Alice, had come to Philadelphia with Howe; Mrs. Pitezel was too ill from nervous prostration to make the long journey. When Howe brought her to the office in the afternoon, Mr. Fouse found her to be fourteen or fifteen years old and rather reticent, embarrassed, and stupid. She corroborated the descriptions of her father given by Holmes and Howe. Mr. Fouse then informed Howe that a Mr. Holmes, who had been Pitezel's employer for some time, was in the city. He asked Howe if he knew Holmes and Howe said he did not. At this point, word was received that Holmes had returned and was in the building. Mr. Fouse asked Howe if he would like to meet him and he said he would.

When Holmes was introduced to Howe, they shook hands and met apparently as strangers. Holmes and Alice did recognize each other, however, and greeted each other on sight. Mr. Fouse suggested that if they were going to exhume the body, they had better agree on marks of identification that would establish it as Pitezel. At this point Howe straightened himself up and said, referring to Holmes, "Who is this man? Why is he here? What is his purpose?" The company president explained the exchange of letters between Cass and Holmes, and Howe said that this was satisfactory.

Holmes mentioned a mole on the back of Pitezel's neck and a scar on his leg. Howe said there was a bruised thumbnail, and Alice agreed. Certain peculiarities of the teeth were also agreed upon, and exhumation was set for the following day, Saturday, September 22.

The exhumation party consisted of Deputy Coroner Dugan, Dr. Mattern, the coroner's physician, a Dr. Hill, President Fouse, his assistant O. Le Forrest Perry, the carpenter-inventor Eugene Smith, Alice Pitezel, attorney Howe, and Holmes. Also present were Doctor Taylor, who was in charge of Potter's Field, and an assistant of his. A number of them had first met at the offices of the insurance company and rode together to the cemetery on a streetcar. It was at that time that Smith tried to strike up a conversation with Holmes. He asked what business he was in, and when Holmes replied, "The patent business, I'm a patent agent," Smith's interest was immediately heightened.

"Well, I have some patents I would like to dispose of, and probably you could do something in the matter," Smith said. Holmes didn't make an offer, so Smith changed the subject.

"How did you come to know that Pitezel was dead?" he now asked. Holmes said he had received a telegram from Mrs. Pitezel. Smith's curiosity was piqued again.

"If you are a patent agent and you travel so much in the United States, how could these people find out where to catch you with a telegram right on the spot?"

Holmes turned, shunning the question of his inquisitive companion, and Smith realized that would be the end of their conversation. He had become more and more certain that this was the same man who had arrived that Monday at Pitezel's house, nodding quickly and walking upstairs. But he couldn't be certain, and he decided to keep his thoughts to himself.

When they arrived at Potter's Field, the coffin had already been removed from its burial ground and placed in a building that served as a toolshed. By now Pitezel's body was a truly repulsive sight, black all over with decomposition, and Alice was spared the ordeal of watching the others examine her father's corpse; Mr. Perry waited with her outside the building. She had begun to cry even before the examination began, with Howe comforting her and joining her in tears, leading Holmes to exclaim that he would pay thirty dollars to have the poor body cremated. He would first have to get permission from the widow, Howe explained.

Dr. Mattern put on his rubber gloves and tore away the garments where the identifying marks were supposed to be, but with the blackened condition of the body, he could distinguish nothing.

13

At this point Holmes took off his coat, rolled up his sleeves, and reached in his pocket and took out a surgeon's gum lancet, similar to Mattern's. He made a mark around the mole, which Doctor Mattern then extracted. Holmes next located the cut on the leg. He and Mattern removed several fingers in search of the bruised nail, but with the blackened color, the bruise would not show until the fingers were placed in alcohol.

The body was now covered so that only the teeth were showing, and Perry brought Alice to the table. "Are these your father's teeth?" he asked, and the sobbing child said yes.

Holmes announced that he wanted to leave town as soon as possible, so on Sunday the coroner, Samuel H. Ashbridge, took his and Alice's sworn statements of identification.

Alice affirmed that "I am in the fifteenth year of my age. Benjamin F. Pitezel was my father. He was thirty-seven years old this year. My mother is living. There are five children. My father came East on July 29th. He left St. Louis. He first went to New York. He left there after August 11th. We learned of his death through the papers. I came on with Mr. Howe to see the body. On Saturday, September 22d, I saw a body at the City Burial Ground and fully recognized the body as that of my father by his teeth. I am fully satisfied that it is he."

Holmes, citing his address as 701 Sixty-third Street, Chicago, stated, "I knew Benjamin F. Pitezel for eight years in Chicago. I had business with him during that time. More recently he had desk room in our office. I received a letter from E.H. Caser [sic], Agent of Fidelity Company, about B. F. Pitezel, he sending a clipping to me. I came to Philadelphia, and saw the body Saturday, September 22d, at the City Burial Ground. I recollected a mole on the back of the neck; a low growth of hair on the forehead; the general shape of the head and his teeth. His daughter Alice had described a scar on the right leg below the knee in front. I found those on the body as described to me by Alice. I have no doubt whatsoever but that it is the body of Benjamin F. Pitezel, who was buried as B. F. Perry. I last saw him alive in November, 1893, in Chicago. I heard he used an assumed name recently, but I never knew him to use any other name than his own before. I found him an honest, honorable man, in all his dealings."

On Monday the officers of the insurance company held a conference and concluded that the identification was satisfactory and complete. They so informed Howe, and he pleaded that Mrs. Pitezel was very poor and sick, with five children to care for. Her husband had left her nothing, said Howe, and he wanted to know how soon the claim could be paid. Howe must have stated his plea with some eloquence for they decided to pay the claim at once, provided the expenses of identifying the body were deducted. Howe agreed reluctantly, and they presented him with a check for $9,715.85. The company also paid Holmes $10 to defray his expenses in coming from Baltimore. Within several weeks the company received letters from Mrs. Pitezel, Alice, Holmes, and Howe, expressing their appreciation for the quick manner in which the claim had been settled.

It must, indeed, be recorded as an unusually prompt and humanitarian gesture on the part of the insurance company. What was never satisfactorily explained later was why the officers of Fidelity Mutual apparently were unconcerned about the possibility of suicide or murder; if it had been suicide, the suicide clause in Pitezel's policy would have voided payment, and murder would have suggested the possibility of conspiracy to gain the claim. Whatever the reasons for their promptness, they soon had reason to repent their action in leisure.

2
NOTED TRAIN ROBBER SQUEALS ON HOLMES

Reveals Plot to Defraud
Fidelity Mutual Insurance.

PLAY THE OLD GAME

Take Out a Policy, Buy a
Cadaver, and Disappear.

HOLMES ARRESTED IN BOSTON

Mrs. Pitezel, After Long Ordeal,
Is Also Placed Under Arrest.

IS PITEZEL ALIVE?

One man at the Fidelity Mutual Life Insurance Company was a determined skeptic, as it was his job to be, for he was William E. Gary, its chief inspector and adjustor. Gary had never completely accepted the evidence that Perry and Pitezel were the same, nor was he satisfied with the conclusion that the man had died accidentally. But when the officers decided to pay the claim, the matter was quickly forgotten.

Several weeks after Jeptha D. Howe departed with his check for $9,715.85, business of a totally unrelated nature brought Inspector Gary to St. Louis. He was in the company's branch office there when he received a message from Maj. Lawrence Harrigan, chief of the St. Louis police. Harrigan said he had received a communication from an inmate of the city prison about an insurance case that Fidelity Mutual had investigated, and he suggested that some officer of the company see him at once.

Without delay, Gary headed for the chief's office. Harrigan handed him a letter he had received from Marion C. Hedgepeth, a prisoner who was awaiting sentence for train robbery. All of Gary's previous suspicions were confirmed when he read that letter, for it exposed an elaborate criminal plot involving Holmes, Howe, and Pitezel, among others.

Marion Hedgepeth, it should be noted, was at the time one of the most notorious criminals in the country, though he never made his mark on the history books—perhaps for lack of a more poetic name. He and his band of ruthless outlaws—known to lawmen as the "Hedgepeth Four"—had successfully stolen $50,000 from a train they stopped near Glendale, Missouri. They made their escape, but were later caught when a young girl accidentally

MARION C. HEDGEPETH.
Photo courtesy of
United Press International.

discovered their hidden guns and money. William A. Pinkerton, who sat on the other side of the law, paid Hedgepeth the distinction of calling him "one of the really bad men of the old West. He was one of the worst characters I ever heard of. He was a bad man clear through." Hedgepeth's trial in 1892 was a national sensation, and he became a folk hero of sorts, receiving so many bouquets of flowers from women admirers that they nearly crowded him from his cell.

As it turned out, H. H. Holmes shared that cell with Marion Hedgepeth in July 1894, when he was charged with swindling in connection with the purchase and sale of a drug store in St. Louis. Holmes, who operated in St. Louis as H. M. Howard, was apparently overwhelmed with awe for the colorful gunfighter who was now his cellmate. There is no other explanation for his indiscretion; perhaps, too, he was anxious to gain Hedgepeth's respect as an equal in criminal conspiracy. It was an indiscretion Holmes would soon regret.

The letter from Marion Hedgepeth to Chief Harrigan deserves reproduction in full, for it spells out the details of Holmes' masterful scheme to defraud the insurance company.

"When H. M. Howard [Holmes] was in here some two months ago," Hedgepeth began, "he came to me and told me he would like to talk to me, as he had read a great deal of me, etc.; also after we got well acquainted, he told me he had a scheme by which he could make $10,000, and he needed some lawyer who could be trusted, and said if I could, he would see that I got $500 for it. I then told him that J. D. Howe could be trusted, and he then went on and told me that B. F. Pitezel's life was insured for $10,000, and that Pitezel and him were going to work the insurance company for the $10,000, and just how they were going to do it; even going into minute details; that he was an expert at it, as he had worked it before, and that being a druggist, he could easily deceive the insurance company by having Pitezel fix himself up according to his directions and appear that he was mortally wounded by an explosion, and then put a corpse in place of Pitezel's body, etc., and then have it identified as that of Pitezel. I did not take much stock in what he told me, until after he went out on bond, which was in a few days, when J. D. Howe came to me and told me that that man Howard, that I had recommended him to, had come and told him that I had recommended Howe to him and had laid the whole plot open to him, and Howe told me that he never heard of a finer or smoother piece of work, and that it was sure to work, and that Howard was one of the smoothest and slickest men that he ever heard tell of, etc., and Howe told me that he would see that I got $500 if it worked, and that Howard was going on East to attend to it at once. (At this time I did not know what insurance company was to be worked, and am not sure yet as to which one it is, but Howe told me that it was the Fidelity Mutual of Philadelphia, whose office is, according to the city directory, at No. 520 Olive Street.) Howe came down and told me every two or three days, that everything was working smoothly and when notice appeared in the *Globe Democrat* and *Chronicle* of the death of B. F. Pitezel, Howe came down at once and told me that it was a matter of a few days until we would have the money, and that the only thing that might keep the company from paying it at once, was the fact that Howard and Pitezel were so hard up for money, that they could not pay the dues on the policy until a day or two before it was due, and then had to send it by telegram, and that the company might claim that they did not get the money until after the lapse of the policy; but they did not, and so Howe and a little girl (I think Pitezel's daughter) went back to Philadelphia and succeeded in identifying and having the body recognized as that of B. F. Pitezel. Howard told me that Pitezel's wife was privy to the whole thing. Howe tells me now that Howard would not let Mrs. Pitezel go back to identify the supposed body of her husband, and

21

that he feels almost positive and certain that Howard deceived Pitezel and that Pitezel in following out Holmes' instructions, was killed and that it was really the body of Pitezel.

"The policy was made out to the wife," Hedgepeth continued, "and when the money was put in the bank, then Howard stepped out and left the wife to settle with Howe for his services. She was willing to pay him $1,000, but he wants $2,500 and so $2,500 of the money is held until they get over squabbling about it. Howard is now on his way to Germany, and Pitezel's wife is here in the city yet, and where Pitezel is or whether that is Pitezel's body I can't tell, but I don't believe it is Pitezel's body, but believe that he is alive and well and probably in Germany, where Howard is now on his way. *It is hardly worth while to say that I never got the $500 that Howard held out to me for me to introduce him to Mr. Howe.* Please excuse this poor writing as I have written this in a hurry and have to write on a book placed on my knee. This and a lot more I am willing to swear to. I wish you would see the Fidelity Mutual Life Insurance Company and see if they are the ones who have been made the victim of this swindle, and if so, tell them that I want to see them. I never asked what company it was until today, and it was after we had some words about the matter, and so Howe may not have told the proper company, but you can find out what company it is by asking or telephoning to the different companies. When I asked Mrs. Pitezel's address he waited a long time and finally said it was No. 6342 S. Michigan Ave. Please send an agent of the company to see me if you please."

Inspector Gary visited Hedgepeth in the city prison, accompanied by a stenographer, and obtained a sworn statement that was in effect a reiteration of what he had revealed in the letter. Hedgepeth added only that Howe, after his return from Philadelphia, now truly believed that the body was Pitezel's, and that Holmes had either murdered him or Pitezel had been killed in an explosion when setting up the job of substitution.

With this sworn statement, Inspector Gary returned to Philadelphia and confronted the company officers with the revelations. Now it was their turn to be skeptical—a tale manufactured by a wily criminal for his own devious purposes, they said. But Gary pointed out aspects of the plot that could not have been known by Hedgepeth unless Howe or Holmes had told him. For one thing, Hedgepeth stated that the premium on the policy had been paid by telegram, and on the very day it was due, August 9. That was known only to the officers of the company and the conspirators, so how could Hedgepeth have known that fact? The company finally agreed to let Inspector Gary make a search for Holmes and, as his work progressed, proof multiplied that they had been made the victim of a swindle. The aid of the Pinkerton detective agency was now secured, and the search for Holmes began in earnest.

*　*　*

The trail of the detectives took them first to Kingston, Ontario, then to Detroit, but without success in locating Holmes in either city. They picked up his trail in Ogdensburg, New York, and followed it to Prescott, Ontario, then Burlington, Vermont, and from there to Tilton and Gilmanton, New Hampshire. In Gilmanton they discovered that Holmes and Howard were both aliases, and that his real name was Herman Webster Mudgett. Moreover, he had been married years earlier to a local girl still living in New Hampshire, whom he never bothered to divorce, making his Wilmette marriage clearly illegal. He was visiting his parents in Gilmanton while under the surveillance of detectives and was shadowed closely as he took a train to Boston.

Fearful that Holmes was going to slip aboard a ship to Europe, the superintendent of the Pinkerton force in Boston, John Cornish, approached Boston police about arresting Holmes on a Philadelphia coroner's warrant charging him with fraud against the insurance company. Deputy Superintendent of Police Orinton M. Hanscom was not satisfied with the warrant, however, and wanted something better to hold him on. By now the investigations of the various detectives on Holmes' trail had revealed that he was also in trouble with the law in Texas. Hanscom wired the authorities in Fort Worth and by return telegram got the warrant he wanted: "Larceny of one horse."

With that, the police closed in and arrested Holmes on the Fort Worth warrant. Meanwhile, Fidelity's O. Le Forrest Perry had arrived in Boston from Philadelphia, and when Holmes saw him enter the police station, he said, "I guess I know what I'm really wanted for." At this time the only crime Holmes was wanted for in Philadelphia was fraud—at least officially; some of the police suspected murder but had no solid evidence with which to proceed. Knowing the refinements of Texas jails and the Texas attitude toward horse thieves,* Holmes readily decided in favor of Philadelphia hospitality and voluntarily confessed to defrauding the insurance company.

From the Rogue's Gallery,
Boston, Mass.

Holmes had rented a house in Burlington, Vermont, where Mrs. Pitezel and two of her children were staying at the time he was arrested. She was lured to Boston by a decoy letter written by the Pinkertons and penned by Holmes, and upon her arrival she too was arrested and placed in the city jail. Meanwhile, the portrait of

*Holmes later wrote to Mrs. Pitezel: "I dislike fearfully to go to Ft. Worth to serve a term, as the prisons there are terrible. I had rather be here [Philadelphia] five years than there one. . . ."

Holmes' personal life continued to grow ever more Byzantine, for at the time of his arrest in Boston he was in the company of Miss Georgiana Yoke, whom he had fraudulently married in Denver under his St. Louis alias of Henry Mansfield Howard. Thus there were now at least three women who thought themselves to be Holmes' wife—one in New Hampshire, one in Wilmette, and Miss Yoke, who soon proved to be entirely honest and an innocent victim of his deceit.

* * *

On November 18 Holmes made his first statement of confession, before Boston's Deputy Superintendent Hanscom and Pinkerton's John Cornish. In it he admitted that a fraud had taken place against the insurance company, but insisted that Pitezel was alive. It was an elaborate, perhaps even plausible story, but as Philadelphia police detective Frank Geyer would later write, "Holmes is greatly given to lying with a sort of florid ornamentation, and all of his stories are decorated with flamboyant draperies, intended by him to strengthen the plausibility of his statements. In talking, he has the appearance of candor, becomes pathetic at times when pathos will serve him best, uttering his words with a quaver in his voice, often accompanied by a moistened eye, then turning quickly with a determined and forceful method of speech, as if indignation or resolution had sprung out of tender memories that had touched his heart." That was a judgment written from bitter experiences months later; for now, Holmes' official audience had no way to judge just how wily and unconscionable their prisoner was.

Holmes began by stating that he had procured a body in New York that was to be represented as Pitezel to the insurance company—the old game of take out a policy, buy a cadaver, and disappear. He had previously instructed Pitezel on what to do with the body, and after placing it in a trunk and delivering it to Philadelphia he returned to New York. Since Pitezel's supposed death he had seen him in Cincinnati and Detroit, but he was evasive when asked to be specific or to give the exact date of the last time he had seen his accomplice: "I cannot give the day. I will leave a blank and fill it in."

Holmes then began spinning an intricate tale of travels throughout the Northeast and Canada, with the Pitezel family split into three groups to avoid detection, Holmes traveling with the girls Alice and Nellie and the boy Howard, Pitezel then splitting off with his son, and Mrs. Pitezel following with her oldest daughter, Dessie, and their baby boy.

Q. It is not really clear to my mind now why the family should be broken up, why the three children should go one way, and she with the two children the other way.

A. The first intention was to have them all go to Cincinnati and stay there for the winter; get a furnished house and have her stay there until any noise might blow over, and he was going into the South on lumber business, and I about my general business. When I got down there I met him. I had the three children, and he had been waiting there some days, and I stayed there with him that night, and the next day, instead of doing as he agreed, he had been drinking a little, and he went and saw the children, which he agreed not to do under any circumstances.

Q. That, of course, gave it away that he was alive?

A. Of course; we could not get them away in a moment.

Q. Your theory was that it was necessary for the three children to accompany him for the safety of the scheme?

A. Well, if the mother knew that they knew, then she would immediately throw it over, as she said, and I think she will tell you so herself.

Q. At the same time, I suppose there was some fear that they might in some way betray the fact that he was still alive?

A. Well, they could not all be together and go to school. You could not depend upon ten- or eleven-year-old children to keep the fact; keep them from speaking among themselves or before strangers; neither could you get them to go under another name and carry it out at that age.

Continuing, Holmes related how Pitezel finally took charge of all three children, freeing him from their care, and sailed with them by boat to the South or to South America. They planned to communicate by cipher in the columns of the Chicago *Tribune* or New York *Herald*, and meanwhile Holmes had to keep Mrs. Pitezel moving by telling her that her husband and other three children were one step ahead of them.

Q. Since delivering the children to him on the outskirts of Detroit you have not seen or heard from him, directly or indirectly?

A. No, sir.

Q. Does his wife know where he is?

A. No, sir.

Q. Has his wife been in search of him lately?

A. Oh, no; because after this break that he made in regard to seeing the children I have had to tell her, while I could get her in shape to send her to him, tell her that he was here and there and put her off.

Q. You have put her off by telling her that her husband was at different points about the country?

A. Yes, sir. . . .

The detectives were also interested in just how involved Mrs. Pitezel was in the plot to defraud the insurance company.

Q. When did Mrs. Pitezel first become acquainted with this scheme?

A. Well, it is pretty hard to tell, because I found out here a week or two ago that her oldest daughter had known of it in the summer, that her father had told her if anything happened to him not to be worried, that he would not be dead, and whether it was the same case with Mrs. Pitezel or not I cannot tell, but my object in

27

leaving Philadelphia a little ahead of when it should come out in the papers was so to get there to sort of break it to her, tell her if she saw it in the papers it was not a fact. Now, to the best of my knowledge and belief that was when she first knew of it.

Q. Did she know from the papers anything about the finding of the body of Perry before you saw her?

A. They found it out in the morning in the papers, that is, the family, the entire family read it and naturally supposed it to be true.

Q. Did it seem to be genuine grief on their part?

A. Yes, sir; the doctor even was called.

Q. Then really you believe that was the first they knew?

A. Yes; this oldest daughter was taking on just as bad as any, and I know now that she knew or supposed it was not really death.

Q. The mother is a rather illiterate, plain person?

A. Yes.

Q. Then you saw her the day that she read this in the paper?

A. The night.

Q. What conversation did you have with her then?

A. I told her then that she need not worry.

Holmes spilled forth in great detail about the arrangements with Jeptha Howe, and where the proceeds from the $10,000 policy had gone. He insisted he could prove that Pitezel was alive after he, Holmes, had left Philadelphia. But when asked to corroborate the story about the cadaver by telling where he got it, Holmes refused.

Q. From whom did you get the body in New York.

A. Well, I have refused thus far to state. I told Mr. Perry I thought I would, but if Pitezel comes up in a few days I would rather not tell that, because I was concerned years ago with this man, in something not exactly of this nature, so intimately that the position he is in, it would hurt him very much. Of course, I will, if it comes right down to saving myself.

Q. I think that while you are telling this thing you should tell the whole truth right as it is. It is a matter that must come out in time, and now is as good a time as any other.

A. . . . . He is a man now well enough to do, so that if my wife becomes penniless, if I am shut up for a term of years, I think I can call upon him for help.

Having finished with Holmes, the Boston authorities now questioned Mrs. Pitezel. They were moved by her pitiable ordeal and desperate situation—here was a plain, unpretentious woman living in poverty with a family of five children, in ill health, and tied by marriage to an alcoholic crook. Her husband and three of her children had disappeared; her remaining two children, one of them just a year old, were without a guardian; and she was in prison, under suspicion of having been a party to a conspiracy to cheat and defraud an insurance company. Nevertheless she was involved to some undetermined extent and her apprehension was unavoidable, even though her punishment outside the law was more than enough to satisfy the sternest demands of justice.

Mrs. Pitezel denied any prior knowledge of the insurance scheme (a position she later recanted) and answered the questions about her travels in search of her husband and children.

Q. He [Holmes] has kept you moving, hasn't he?
A. Yes.
Q. I wish to ask you one question direct. Do you believe now that your husband is alive?
A. Well, there must be something in it. I am sure I could not swear to it for I don't know for a fact that he is alive. All I know is, what you have been telling me, and what he has been telling me, and that is all I know.
Q. But he has kept you moving from point to point; I would like to have you tell it in your own way.
A. Well, I have been moving from one point to another. I have been just heartbroken, that is all there is about it.
. . . .
Q. Have you had confidence in Howard [Holmes] all

29

the way through, that he would finally take you to your husband?

A. Why, I thought so.

Q. Has your confidence ever been shaken?

A. Well, sometimes I thought maybe he was fooling me or something.

. . . .

Q. We are not doing anything to undertake to make you feel bad, we are trying to get at the matter and sift it. He has kept you moving about the country from point to point, and you look as though you had been through a good deal and we want to get all the light we can. We don't believe in this man very much. That is why we are asking you these questions.

A. Do you know where the children are?

Q. No, that is one of the things we want to find out. We want to find them as much for your sake, as for any other reason in the world. In fact, we may say that all these questions that are being asked you now regarding these children are in your behalf. Holmes is locked up in this very building, and we have been talking with him.

A. *I thought maybe I would see my children here.*

* * *

On Monday, November 19, 1894, Philadelphia police detective Thomas G. Crawford arrived in Boston with warrants for the arrest of Holmes and Mrs. Pitezel. Both of them, however, agreed to go without the formality of a requisition from the governor of Pennsylvania. Returning by train to Philadelphia were Detective Crawford, Mr. Perry of the insurance company, Holmes, Miss Yoke, Mrs. Pitezel, and her two children.

In conversation while handcuffed to Crawford, Holmes laughed at the way Pitezel supposedly bungled the job, and asked if he believed in hypnotism. Crawford said no. Holmes said he could hypnotize people very easily and demonstrated the sort of hypnotism in which he was most proficient by offering to give the

detective $500 for a purpose not stated, but quite well understood.
"Hypnotism," returned the detective, "always spoils my appetite. I'm afraid the $500 is no inducement when weighed against possible dyspepsia."

On Tuesday the train pulled into Philadelphia's Central Station, and the two prisoners were escorted to City Hall. There they were given a hearing and were at once committed to prison to await trial. Dessie Pitezel and the baby were placed in the custody of Benjamin Crew, secretary of the Society to Protect Children from Cruelty. Within a few days Jeptha Howe was brought from St. Louis and held in $2,500 bail. The office of District Attorney George S. Graham then indicted H. H. Holmes, Benjamin F. Pitezel, Carrie A. Pitezel, and Jeptha D. Howe with having fraudulently and willfully conspired to cheat and defraud the Fidelity Mutual Life Association of the sum of $10,000, by means of the substitution of a body for that of Benjamin F. Pitezel.

Eventually this indictment would be presented to a grand jury, and Holmes would plead guilty on the second day of the trial. For now, there was much speculation, but as yet no proof, that Pitezel had been killed by his senior partner in crime. "This is the belief," reported Chicago's *Inter Ocean*, "not only of the detectives of the Fidelity Insurance Company, which was so cleverly victimized, but of Superintendent of Police Linden and the coroner."

Alexander McKnight, a vice-president of the insurance firm, told the press that "while the suspicion has grown until we are nearly positive that B. F. Pitezel was murdered, the only charge made before the grand jury was that of conspiracy to defraud."

Coroner Ashbridge was just as positive that the corpse discovered at 1316 Callowhill Street was B. F. Pitezel. "I am not at liberty at present to disclose my reasons for this assertion," he told reporters, "but if I were, and pointed them out, you would be convinced, notwithstanding the stories as to the wretched man's expatriation in South America or elsewhere, that he met his death right here in Philadelphia."

3

CONSTERNATION
IN CHICAGO

H. H. Holmes, the Alleged
Insurance Swindler,
Well Known in This City.

FINDS EASY PREY

Swindled With Dash and Vim
and Had Victims Untold.

READS LIKE ROMANCE

Begins His Chicago Career
by Building a "Castle" With
Other People's Money.

FOND OF THE SOCIETY OF WOMEN

When H. H. Holmes was arrested in Boston, a remarkable career of fraud and crime was brought to a close. While he worked his schemes over a wide territory all the way from Texas to New England, Chicago appeared to have been especially favored by the young man. His career, said the Chicago *Herald*, "stamps him as one of the boldest and shrewdest swindlers in the country. He left scores of victims in Chicago, where firms and individuals right and left were swindled out of various sums through all sorts of fantastic methods. . . . He swindled with a dash and vim that must have won the admiration almost of those who lost."

Holmes' favorite method of raising money in a hurry was to buy something on time and sell it the same day or the next for cash. It is not recorded that he ever paid for anything except the life insurance policies he used for fraudulent ends. The day after the newspapers carried the story of his arrest, more than fifty persons called at Chicago's central police station and inquired after Holmes. All had been swindled by him.

Apparently he first arrived in Chicago around 1886, when he was but twenty-six years old. Holmes claimed to be a graduate of the medical school at Ann Arbor, Michigan, and he encountered no difficulty in obtaining a position as clerk in the drug store owned by Mrs. E. S. Holton, whose husband had recently died. Her pharmacy was located at the corner of Sixty-third and Wallace streets in Englewood, a fashionable and fast-growing suburban neighborhood on the South Side of Chicago.* Holmes soon proved to have a pleasing way with customers, especially the

*See Appendix I: Holmes' Englewood.

35

female ones, and business prospered. In a few months Mrs. Holton and her young daughter disappeared. Holmes told his customers that she had sold him the business and moved away. She was never seen again.

The ambitious Holmes would not be satisfied until he had his own building and was able to expand into other fields of business as well. A double lot across the corner at 701 and 703 Sixty-third Street was vacant and available, and Holmes secured a lease of the land, paying mostly in conversational pyrotechnics. On it he began the erection of a two-story brick building, paid for, one might say, with borrowed capital and wind, and quickly dubbed "the Holmes castle" because of the battlements on the street fronts of the building. When it was completed, the building was buried under mechanics' liens and mortgages. From Morrisson, Plummer & Co., wholesale druggists, Holmes got $2,500 and a stock of drugs. He gave them a mortgage on the building but asked them to wait a few days before having the mortgage recorded. They waited. The next day Holmes deeded the property to a woman in Minneapolis, believed to be a myth. At the time of his arrest, seven years later, the druggists still had not recovered their money and the matter was still in litigation. The property was deeded from one person to another, ostensibly, but creditors could never find anyone claiming to be the owner. Meanwhile, Holmes lived upstairs over the drug store and collected rents.

Holmes furnished the building in the same way as he constructed it. Before he was finished, goods worth a small fortune, but not paid for, had been brought to his scene of operations. Most of these goods were sold and resold and little was ever recovered by the original owners.

When the Tobey Furniture Company became suspicious that all was not right, they sent a man to Holmes' building but he was unable to find any of the goods they had sold on credit. A porter from the store was more successful. He found a construction man working around the place and opened negotiations for some information. They agreed upon fifty dollars as the price of the correct tip as to where the goods could be found.

The construction worker led the representatives of the Tobey Company into a vacant room and, feeling along the wall, showed

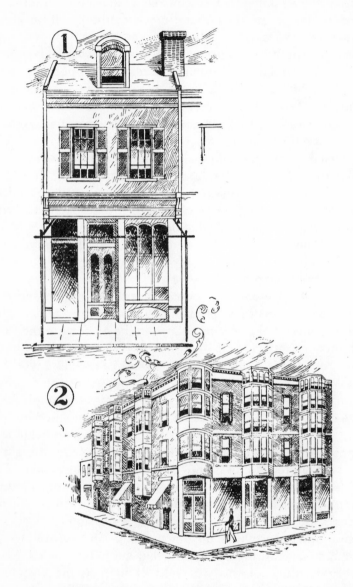

1.—1316 Callowhill Street, Philadelphia, where B. F. Pitezel met his death.

2.—Holmes "Castle" on Sixty-Third Street in Chicago.

them where to cut through the wallpaper and the thin partition under it. By so doing they discovered a hidden door leading into a secret room, where they found much of the furniture obtained from them and a great amount of goods from other concerns. There was another entrance to this room, but it was a devious one. There was a freight elevator in the rear of the building, and by stopping this elevator midway between the two floors and removing a few boards, access could be gained to the secret room.

Of course Holmes had to have a safe. He bought a large one on time before the building was finished and put it in a room not half completed. When the safe makers came for their money, Holmes said to them, "I have none; take back the safe."

The men went after it but quickly learned there wasn't a door or a window in the room large enough for the safe to pass through. Holmes' attention was called to the fact.

"Take the safe," repeated the druggist, "but I warn you not to mar the building."

The safe stayed put.

In 1892 Englewood was booming with apartment and board-inghouse construction in preparation for the tremendous influx of visitors expected the coming year with the opening of the World's Columbian Exposition. Holmes was not idle. He planned to add a third story to his building, which would be used as a world's fair hotel. At this time the building was supposedly owned by the "Campbell-Yates Manufacturing Company." "Campbell" was none other than B. F. Pitezel and Holmes represented himself as agent for the company, whose other incorporators were a Miss Minnie Williams, Holmes' typewriter,* Henry Owens, a porter who worked for Holmes, and "A. S. Yates," whom, like "Campbell," nobody ever saw. On the credit of the fictitious Hiram S. Campbell, Holmes visited brick men, contractors, furniture dealers, and others and obtained their goods and services. In due time another story was on the building, and furnishings for a structure several times its size had been contracted for and delivered. Much of this was sold as soon as the wagons that delivered it were driven away.

*That is, his secretary, or stenographer.

Most of these operations were negotiated merely by Holmes' presentation of a letter purporting to be signed by H. S. Campbell, the supposed money man of the concern, giving Holmes authority to purchase such goods as he desired. Anyone questioning the reliability of "H. S. Campbell" was referred to Wharton Plummer, an attorney with an office in the Chamber of Commerce Building. Those who checked with Plummer came away satisfied that Campbell owned at least $40,000 worth of real estate in Cook County. Of course, none of the people with whom he had business dealings were ever able to find "Mr. Campbell," although he was supposed to be in Chicago for the world's fair. Whenever anyone asked to see him they were informed that he had "just stepped out."

Holmes would get two bicycles from every bicycle company with which he came in contact. He would lease the wheels, giving as security notes for large amounts signed by the ever serviceable Mr. Campbell; then he would quickly sell the bicycles. He juggled in similar fashion with cash registers, brick, lumber, furniture, gas fixtures, and anything else he could get hold of.

Holmes was too much of an entrepreneur by now to be restricted to running the drug store. When A. L. Jones drifted in from northern Michigan, he thought the location a good one and made an offer for the store. It was accepted. The deal was closed one Saturday night, but Jones was not to take possession until the following Monday. On Sunday Holmes sold all the costly manicure sets and toilet articles and pocketed the proceeds. Jones didn't prosecute for some reason or another. He even kept quiet when some men came around a few days later and carted off the soda fountain, a handsome affair worth about $1,500, but of course not paid for. Jones finally got tired and sold out.

We will never know just how many business fronts Holmes had operating from his property, or how many legitimate business and professional men rented space there. A business directory published in 1891 placed offices of commission merchants Gregson & Fischer at 703 Sixty-third Street.* The city directory for 1887 listed Holmes' drug store and carried his advertisement for

*See, again, Appendix I: Holmes' Englewood.

"Drugs, Paints and Oils. Linden Grove Mineral Spring Water." The 1889 directory listed a barber shop operated by Holmes at 6304 Wallace Street, which would be on the other front of the building, and the following year Holmes was registered as manager of the Warner Glass Bending Company at 701 Sixty-third Street. The 1890 directory also listed a Dr. Henry D. Mann at that address, with no hint, of course, whether this was a legitimate physician renting an office or still another alias for Holmes. Holmes also started a restaurant at number 703, and once sold it to an Aurora man named Phillips for $900 down. Everything in the restaurant was taken away from Phillips by the men who had sold the furnishings to Holmes on time. Holmes was said to have played this restaurant game whenever hard pressed for $1,000 or so.

Some of Holmes' schemes for turning a quick profit were quite comical— if you were not his partner in the business relationship. One of them was novel and successful. In the basement under the drug store Holmes placed a galvanized iron tank. Into the tank he threw a lot of old junk and chemicals that created strange colors and stranger odors. Then he tapped a gas main, ran a pipe through the tank and up into the store, and burned the gas.

"See," he would say to his friends, "I make my own gas, and it is just as good as any in the city."

A visiting Canadian looked at the bright jets in the store, at the strange-smelling tank, and then paid Holmes $2,000 for the "patent." The Canadian was said to have died of a broken heart instead of sending Holmes to the penitentiary. Holmes was believed to have arranged a settlement with the gas company.

Just as novel was his "artesian well," from which he obtained his water supply for the store. This was the "Linden Grove Mineral Spring Water" that he advertised and sold over the counter for five cents a cup, his customers going away convinced that it did wonders for whatever ailed them. Holmes said the "well" was in the basement. The city water department took no stock in this story, and men were sent to dig up the earth in Sixty-third Street, along which the water mains ran, to see if they had been tapped. The mains were found intact. Weeks ran along and so did the "artesian well." The water men made another attack on the mains with the same result. Finally they visited Holmes a third time, with instructions now to dig all around the block if necessary. Then it was discovered that Holmes had gone to the rear and crossed over to a north-and-south main in order to tap for his water supply. But again he escaped punishment in some way.

Not all of the schemes were successful, even for Holmes. In the summer of 1893 he insured the building and its contents for $21,000, and a few weeks later the roof caught fire in some mysterious fashion. The loss was estimated by the adjustors at $5,500. The insurance company became suspicious and engaged Charles B. Obermeyer, an attorney, and Thiel's Detective Agency to investigate. The insurance was in Campbell's name, but Holmes tried to collect as agent. When Holmes' unsavory activities were noted by the detective agency, the attorney's advice to the insurance company was to pay the claim to nobody but Campbell. Campbell could not be produced, of course, and the insurance was never paid.

*   *   *

When the Holmes-Pitezel case hit the front pages of the newspapers, associates and neighbors in Englewood began to talk about their impressions and recollections of the men. One of the most loquacious was C. E. Davis, who ran the jewelry section of Holmes' drug store.

"Holmes liked to have young women for clerks," he recalled, "and while he assumed to keep them on the jewelry side of the store they used sometimes to have to cross the floor to the drug counter, where he was, for change or something. Mrs. Holmes [presumably the Wilmette one] noticed this and probably said something about it. After that he rigged up an electric bell in connection with a loose board near the top of the stairs leading from his flat overhead to the store, so he might be early apprised of his spouse's coming down. It was noticeable that when that bell rang he was the busiest man in Englewood.

"Holmes was lavish with money when he could get it," Davis continued. "He must have made $200,000 while he was here, but I believe it is all gone. In fact, from what I know of the man I am inclined to believe that he would never have attempted this alleged insurance fraud if he had not been very hard up. But I don't believe it was a fraud in the sense of the dispatches. I should not be surprised if that was Pitezel's body that was burned and if Holmes knew all about his death."

Where, then, did Mrs. Pitezel fit in?

"It looks to me as if Mrs. Pitezel was 'standing in' with the scheme. One thing I know. Holmes used to give her money. You see, he frequently got drafts for considerable amounts, and as he was afraid to put his money in a bank on account of his credit-

C. E. DAVIS,
who ran the jewelry section of Holmes' drug store. From the *Chicago Times-Herald*, July 25, 1895, p. 2. Courtesy of the Illinois State Historical Library.

ors, he would have me bank it for him and then get me to draw checks for him when he needed cash. Well, I have had more than several checks come back to me indorsed by Mrs. Pitezel, so he surely gave her money."

Davis noted that "Holmes was prone to spend money in only one direction, so far as I know. He never gambled, smoked or drank. He was the smoothest man I ever saw. Why, I have known creditors to come here raging and calling him all the names imaginable, and he would smile and talk to them and set up the cigars and drinks and send them away seemingly his friends for life. I never saw him angry. You couldn't have trouble with him if you tried."

By now Davis was warming to his subject, and the awe in which he held his charlatan of an employer was evident.

"I'll give you a sample of the man. Nearly every particle of material in this building and its fixtures was got on credit and very little of it was ever paid for. If all the writs of mechanic's lien that have been levied on this structure were pasted on these three walls, the block would look like a mammoth circus billboard. But I never heard of a lien being collected. Holmes used to tell me he had a lawyer paid to keep him out of trouble, but it always seemed to me that it was the courteous, audacious rascality of the fellow that pulled him through. One day he bought some furniture for his restaurant and moved it in, and that very evening the dealer came around to collect his bill or remove the goods. Holmes set up the drinks, took him to supper, bought him a cigar and sent the man off laughing at a joke, with a promise to call the next week for his money. In thirty minutes after he took his car Holmes had wagons in front loading up that furniture and the dealer never got a cent. Holmes didn't go to jail, either. He was the only man in the United States that could do what he did. I believe he was an English crook who had found the old country too hot for him."

Pitezel's appearance on the scene was also recalled in Englewood. His old neighbors described him as more than willing to aid Holmes in his unique ventures, but lacking the cool and polished effrontery of the senior partner. "It is about five years since Pitezel came to Chicago," said Robert Latimer, gatekeeper at Wallace and Sixty-third streets. "Holmes was putting up his building then, and Pitezel succeeded me in charge of the horses, and he did some carpenter work, too. There was a story in the neighborhood that he had been put in jail in Indiana on a charge of forgery and that Holmes had bailed him out, and that he had then jumped his bail. I never heard him deny it."

Holmes and Pitezel disappeared from Englewood at the same time, escaping the growing army of creditors and seeking their fortune in Texas and St. Louis for a while. From that time until Holmes' arrest in Boston, there was only one report of them returning to the old neighborhood. Dr. E. H. Robinson, one of Holmes' tenants and successors in the drug store, ran into Holmes on Van Buren Street near the river, disguised and trying to avoid recognition. Finding himself known, however, Holmes tried to turn the encounter to his advantage by telling Dr. Robinson he was in sore straits for money and would give him three months' rent for two months' payment in hand. Robinson refused. This was about the time they took out the policy on Pitezel's life, and Robinson now assumed they had wanted the money to pay the premiums. On the same day that Holmes was seen on Van Buren Street, Pitezel came to the store and talked with jeweler Davis.

"Holmes and Pitezel are not seriously missed in Englewood," reported the Chicago *Herald*. "Most of their Chicago creditors are in the downtown district. Dealers in the neighborhood of Wallace and Sixty-third streets soon found out his peculiar notions of debit and credit and finally refused to let his name go into their books. Hence except for a few little bills for household supplies, Englewood withers are unwrung and the community is free to rejoice that Holmes got away when he did."

There was a similar lack of grief over Holmes' plight among his neighbors in the northern suburb of Wilmette. It was here that Holmes established the family residence with his second wife, the former Myrta Z. Belknap, whom he married under the name of Henry Howard Holmes. Holmes had met her in Minneapolis, where her father worked for a railroad company and she was a clerk in a music store. The Belknaps moved to Wilmette in 1889, and the Holmeses joined them several years later. They lived together in a comfortable two-story red frame house on John Street, between Central and Lake avenues, and next to the Congregational church; it was a pretty part of an attractive suburb.

Wilmette residence of H. H. Holmes. From the *Chicago Daily Tribune*, July 25, 1895, p. 2.

Holmes was not popular among his neighbors there, though he could not have spent too much time at home, judging from his extensive travels and his activities on Sixty-third Street. Everyone said Holmes was a "smart" man, but of the type of smartness that is expensive to those who have dealings with him. Myrta had a brother, John, who worked as driver of an express wagon about the village. John used to talk a great deal about the family affairs, it was said, until frequent drubbings drilled it into the youngster that he must keep his mouth shut.

Mrs. Myrta Holmes' initial reactions were to defend her besieged husband. A tall, attractive woman with light hair and eyes, she remained self-possessed and seemed not in the least disturbed by the headlines.

"Naturally I know a great deal of Mr. Holmes' business," she told reporters. "I do not intend to be interviewed about it, for it is his business and no one else's. I have no doubt he will clear himself of all accusations if given a fair opportunity," she added, with emphasis on the word "fair." "Every business man has enemies, and Mr. Holmes has some who would like to overwhelm him."

The second Mrs. Holmes did shed some light on their domestic life before she dismissed the press. "As for having another wife," she began, "I do not believe it. I have the utmost confidence in him. Our domestic relations have been pleasant, and so far as there being any separation I have never heard of such a thing. Mr. Holmes left the first of January. He has been here twice since then on brief visits, and I was with him during the winter on one of his business trips to the south. We have one child, a little daughter, and have been married about nine years. Mr. Pitezel was his business partner at one time, I believe. I hear from my husband two and three times a week and he continually sends me money for my needs and wants. That does not look like there being trouble between us, does it? And as for other matters Mr. Holmes can answer for himself. I have nothing to add."

Despite her brave front with the press, Myrta Holmes must have suspected that there was some truth to the charges against her husband, for on at least one occasion he had exploited a personal friend of hers for sha-dowy ends. That friend was Miss Kate Durkee, who lived with her brother William in Omaha. Myrta and Kate had been child-hood friends in Pennsylvania, and had corresponded ever since their families separated. Each

LUCY,
Holmes' young daughter by Myrta Z. Belknap. From the *Chicago Daily Tribune*, July 26, 1895, p. 2.

year Kate and her brother returned to Pennsylvania for a family visit, and after Myrta's marriage to Holmes they made it a point to travel by way of Chicago and stay over a day with them, on both the outward and return trips. They did not see much of Holmes, whose business seemed to keep him away most of the time, but when he was at home he was a perfect host and gentleman. He did have one characteristic that detracted from their good opinion of him, however, and that was his inability to look a person squarely in the eye.

On one of their visits, Holmes took Miss Durkee and her brother to a large plant where he manufactured a letter copier called the "A.B.C. Copier"—apparently one of the few legitimate businesses Holmes was ever involved with. Mr. Durkee had such confidence in the product that he tried to interest the railroad for which he worked. Holmes appeared to be enjoying a prosperous business, having contracts with large concerns; one which Mr. Durkee saw was with the government. The income from that plant, William thought, must be fully $4,000 a month.

Sometime afterwards Miss Durkee happened to be visiting the Holmes residence without her brother. "Dr. Holmes came to me," she recalled, "and asked me if he could not place his property in my name, as he could not hold it. During the visits to Holmes I had become pretty well acquainted with the doctor, and as he was such a polished, polite gentleman and such a good husband and father, providing his family with everything that would contribute to their happiness, I acquiesced in his request. He explained at the time that it was only a matter of form, and being ignorant of business affairs, I accepted his statement as being true. The property was deeded to me and I never had the deed recorded.

"Some time afterward," she continued, "Dr. Holmes came and requested me to have him appointed as my administrator, so that he could handle the property as he wanted to. I did so, and at his request deeded the property to a man in Chicago named Campbell, but I do not know who he is nor what was his occupation. After this I began thinking that there was something suspicious, but I had such confidence in the husband of my friend that I didn't think he was capable of doing wrong. After this Dr. Holmes sent me some stock in some enterprise in which he was interested, asking me to keep it for him awhile."

Then came a rude shock for the innocent lady: a deposition filed by creditors of Holmes. The entire transaction, of course, had been a ruse to keep them from gaining control of his property in Chicago. When the lawyer for the creditors interviewed her, he realized that she had been used by Holmes, as had so many others, and she escaped with nothing more than the personal hurt inflicted by the husband of her dear friend.

"I have since visited the family in Chicago," she told reporters, "but he never again mentioned anything about his business affairs and appeared to be quite reticent regarding his business, especially in the presence of his family. . . . I still have some of the correspondence relating to the transactions I had with him and will look it up. I thought on several occasions that I would destroy those letters, but something impelled me not to do it. This is positively all I know in relation to Dr. Holmes and his transactions, and I feel as if he has taken advantage of my ignorance and friendship and used me for a stool pigeon to further his schemes."

4
A NEW CONFESSION FROM HOLMES

Says Pitezel a Suicide;
the Children in London
with M. Williams,
His Former Typewriter.

ANOTHER FABRICATION?

Police Put Detective Geyer
on Trail of Children.

HE FACES GREAT ODDS

As Holmes languished in jail, he gradually came to realize the extent of his predicament. He had voluntarily confessed to fraud, knowing from his attorneys that Pennsylvania law placed a maximum prison sentence of two years for conspiracy to defraud. But Mrs. Pitezel, as soon as she arrived in Philadelphia, had decided to tell the police all that she knew, this time without reservations and with complete honesty and sincerity. Moreover, there were gaps and contradictions in the confession he had made in Boston, and the police had noted some of these. From the newspaper accounts he read in his cell, he realized that virtually nobody believed that Pitezel was alive and in South America. Everyone assumed that it was his body, indeed, that was found at 1316 Callowhill, and the district attorney's office and police were busy establishing the fact—and Holmes' complicity in the matter. It was time, therefore, to cover his tracks as best as he could, and on December 27, 1894, Holmes wrote to Superintendent of Police Linden and asked if he could see him. Permission was granted.

Holmes told the police chief that he was very sorry he had lied in his statement of confession and in subsequent statements. He was now ready to tell the truth, the whole truth, and nothing but the truth. A stenographer was brought in, and Holmes began dictating what the police called "Confession No. 2."

In this new rendition, Holmes admitted visiting the Callowhill Street house three or four times. He found Pitezel despondent and drinking heavily, he claimed, and on Saturday Pitezel came to the house where Holmes was boarding and told him that his baby was sick in St. Louis, and he must return home. "I raised no objection to his going." Pitezel needed money for the trip, though, and Holmes said he couldn't arrange for that until the following day.

51

On Sunday morning, around half-past ten, Holmes let himself into the house but didn't find Pitezel on either the first or second floor. He did some reading at the library, then returned to the house. Still no Pitezel. But as Holmes went to Pitezel's desk to write some letters, he noticed a scrap of paper with a figure cipher on it that the two sometimes used. Decoded, it said: "Get letter out bottle in cupboard." In the letter, his friend and associate announced his intention to commit suicide and said he could be found on the top floor of the house.

Holmes ran up, he said, and found Pitezel on the floor apparently dead, the stench of chloroform filling the room. He quickly decided he would have to make it appear as though it was an explosion, for if it was a suicide they would get no money from the insurance company. He brought the body down to the second-story room where it was later found—Holmes gave no reason for this transfer—and smashed a bottle containing benzine, chloroform, and ammonia. He took some of this fluid and splashed it over Pitezel's face and upper body, then set fire to it and left the house as fast as he could.

Holmes' second confession was believed about as much as the first, and it created a new problem as well. The indictment on which he was being held charged Holmes with having *substituted* a body, and if it truly was Pitezel their indictment would not meet the case. A new indictment was found, therefore, and it charged H. H. Holmes, Marion C. Hedgepeth, and Jeptha D. Howe with having conspired to cheat the insurance company by alleging that Pitezel had died *as the result of an accident.* This language was ingeniously constructed to meet the facts of the case within the grasp of the commonwealth. It would be valid if a body had been substituted and Pitezel was alive; it would be valid if Pitezel had committed suicide; and it would be equally valid if Pitezel had been murdered.

On June 3, 1895, Holmes was tried under this new indictment. His counsel informed him that a conviction for conspiracy would bring him a two-year sentence at most, and if he pleaded guilty, he might get off with less. Holmes readily agreed to plead guilty and did so on the second day of the trial. The judge said he would not sentence him then but would consider his case at a later date, and

Holmes appeared happy and confident. But in that courtroom, observing him, were two people who would uncover what he now assumed he had successfully concealed. One was Thomas W. Barlow, an attorney retained by the insurance company, now to be appointed special assistant district attorney. The other was Frank P. Geyer, for twenty years a trusted member of the Philadelphia police department's detective bureau, with vast experience in murder cases. They would soon begin the great work of uncovering one of the greatest criminals of the day.

* * *

As Holmes talked cheerfully with his counsel, word came to him that the district attorney had requested a conference in his office. Holmes was escorted into the room, and he and his counsel were seated on one side of a long table. On the other side were Mr. Graham and Mr. Barlow.

District Attorney Graham began by informing Holmes that he was dismissing any further charges against Mrs. Pitezel, since she had suffered enough. But she was in danger of losing her reason over the uncertainty of the fate of Alice, Nellie, and Howard, and the officers of the commonwealth were most anxious to find the children and return them to their mother.

"It is strongly suspected, Holmes," said Graham, "that you have not only murdered Pitezel, but that you have killed the children. The best way to remove this suspicion is to produce the children at once. Now where are they? Where can I find them? Tell me and I will use every means in my power to secure their early recovery. . . . You were arrested in November and you said the children were with their father in South America. It is now May, and we have heard nothing of them. . . . I am almost persuaded that your word cannot be depended upon, yet I am not averse to giving you an opportunity to assist me in clearing up the mystery which surrounds their disappearance and their present abode, and I now ask you to answer frankly and truthfully, Where are the children?"

Holmes listened quietly and attentively, then answered with every appearance of candor.

"The last time I saw Howard," he said, "was in Detroit, Michigan. There I gave him to Miss Williams [Holmes' former typewriter in Chicago], who took him to Buffalo, New York, from which point she proceeded to Niagara Falls. After the departure of Howard, in Miss Williams' care, I took Alice and Nellie to Toronto, Canada, where they remained for several days. At Toronto I purchased railroad tickets for them for Niagara Falls, put them on the train, and rode out of Toronto with them a few miles, so that they would be assured that they were on the right train. Before their departure, I prepared a telegram which they should send me from the Falls, if they failed to meet Miss Williams and Howard, and I also carefully pinned in the dress of Alice, four hundred dollars in large bills, so Miss Williams would be in funds to defray their expenses.

"They joined Miss Williams and Howard at Niagara Falls," Holmes continued, "from which point they went to New York City. At the latter place, Miss Williams dressed Nellie as a boy, and took a steamer for Liverpool, whence they went to London. If you search among the steamship offices in New York, you must search for a woman and a girl and two boys, and not a woman and two girls and a boy. This was all done to throw the detectives off the track, who were after me for the insurance fraud. Miss Williams opened a massage establishment at No. 80 Veder or Vadar Street, London. I have no doubt the children are with her now, and very likely at that place."

Holmes was almost tearful as he denied with great emphasis that he had killed Pitezel or the children: "Why should I kill innocent children?" Then Mr. Barlow asked, "Please give me the name of one respectable person to whom I can go, either in Detroit, Buffalo, Toronto, Niagara Falls, or New York, who will say that they saw Miss Williams and the three children together." This question staggered Holmes for a moment, but he quickly recovered and said in an injured tone that the question implied a disbelief in his statement. He was promptly told that it certainly did.

Protesting again, Holmes said that he and Miss Williams had made arrangements to communicate by means of a cipher code placed in the personal column of the New York *Herald*. He was

ALICE PITEZEL.

NELLIE PITEZEL.

HOWARD PITEZEL.

55

told to prepare a cipher that would get a response from Miss Williams, and accordingly the personal column of the June 2, 1895, *Herald* carried this advertisement:

MINNIE WILLIAMS, ADELE COVELLE, GERALDINE WAN-DA.—AplbenRun nb CBRc EBLbrB 10th PREeB ABnucu PCAeUcBu RubuPB. Also write pk PRaaAB cbepBa. Address, GEORGE S. GRAHAM, City Hall, Philadelphia, Penn., U.S.A.

This message, said Holmes, would be translated by Miss Williams to read:

IMPORTANT TO HEAR BEFORE 10TH. CABLE. RETURN CHILDREN AT ONCE. ALSO WRITE MR. MASSIE [Miss Williams' former guardian]. HOLMES. [Address, etc.]

Although no one in the district attorney's office believed this latest story from Holmes, they could not afford to pass up any opportunity to discover what had happened to the children. But there was no answer to the ad; there was no record of Miss Williams and the children in London; in fact, there was not even a listing in London for a Veder or Vadar Street.

The children had disappeared in October 1894, and it was now June 1895. With such a lapse of time, what clues could they hope to uncover? After Holmes had been arrested in Boston, insurance company detectives had traced the path of the children to Cincinnati, Indianapolis, Chicago, and then Detroit. At that point Howard disappeared. Holmes and the two girls were then traced to Toronto, where they disappeared. On the surface, therefore, the previous investigations appeared to substantiate Holmes' new story of giving Howard to Miss Williams in Detroit and sending the girls to her from Toronto. But Holmes read the newspapers regularly in his cell, and from them he knew that the detectives had established these paths. He merely adjusted the story to fit the new situation.

A few important clues, however, had not been reported. When Holmes was arrested, a tin box was found that contained ten or twelve letters from Alice and Nellie to their mother and grand-parents,* and a number of letters written by Mrs. Pitezel to the children; these apparently were supposed to have been mailed by Holmes and were not. They would now provide valuable leads to Detective Geyer, as would a small bunch of keys found by Miss Yoke in her trunk and surrendered by her to the police.

On June 19, Mrs. Pitezel was released from prison. On that very same day she received a remarkable letter from Holmes, in which he pleaded that "I was as careful of the children as if they were my own, and you know me well enough to judge me better than strangers here can do. Ben would not have done anything against me, or I against him, any quicker than brothers. We *never* quarrelled. Again, he was worth too much to me for me to have killed him, if I had no other reason not to. As to the children, I never will believe, until you tell me so yourself, that you think they are dead or that I did anything to put them out of the way. Knowing me as you do, can you imagine me killing little and innocent children, especially without any motive?" Somehow the word "especially" introducing that last clause sounded ominous.

It was against staggering odds, therefore, that Detective Geyer left Philadelphia on June 26 in search of the fate of the children. The insurance company gladly provided funds to defray the expenses of the search, though they were pessimistic about un-covering any answers. District Attorney Graham and his assistant, Mr. Barlow, refused to succumb to pessimism, however. A criminal always makes some blunder between the inception and the consummation of his crime, and if any man could unravel Holmes' blunders, it was Detective Frank Geyer.

*The text of some of these touching letters is provided in Appendix II: A Holmes Chronology.

5
CHILDREN'S BLOOD SHED

Bodies of Two Pitezel Girls
Discovered in Toronto Cellar.

SAD SCENE IN MORGUE

Mrs. Pitezel Identifies the
Corpses of Her Children.

HOWARD PITEZEL'S FATE
JUST AS TRAGIC

His Bones Found in the Chimney
of a Cottage Near Indianapolis.

HOLMES SILENT

When Detective Geyer left Philadelphia, he took with him photographs of Holmes and every member of the Pitezel family. He also had photographs of three trunks—one belonging to Miss Yoke (Mrs. Howard), a missing trunk that belonged to the children, and a trunk of Mrs. Pitezel's that Holmes borrowed in Detroit, saying he wanted it for the purpose of getting Ben out of town, as the detectives were onto him.

Geyer's first destination was Cincinnati, where he enlisted the aid of an old friend on the police force, Detective John Schnooks. Geyer knew that Holmes had left St. Louis on September 28 with Nellie and Howard and that they would be joined by Alice, so he suggested to Schnooks that they first check the registers of hotels in the vicinity of the depots. After a number of unsuccessful inquiries, the clerk of a cheap hotel called the Atlantic House produced a registration entry on September 28 for an Alex E. Cook and three children. They had stayed one night, and he thought they resembled the photographs produced by Geyer. More inquiries showed that they registered the following night at the Hotel Bristol, as A. E. Cook and three children from Cleveland.

Knowing that Holmes was in the habit of renting houses in nearly every city that he visited, Geyer and Schnooks began checking with real estate agents. Holmes had indeed rented a house from one of them, at 305 Poplar Street, paying fifteen dollars in advance for it and giving the name of A. C. Hayes. The detectives went there and talked to the next-door neighbor, a Miss Hill, who was more than willing to tell all that she had observed. She had seen a furniture wagon arrive at the house on a Saturday

Detective Frank P. Geyer.

morning, with a man and a small boy getting off. After the man removed a key from his pocket and opened the door, a large, iron cylinder stove, such as was used in barrooms or a large hall, was hauled out of the wagon and into the house. As no other furniture was brought in, her curiosity was aroused and she spoke of it to a number of her neighbors. Holmes apparently observed her, for the following morning he rang her bell and announced that he would not be occupying the house, and she could have the stove.

Geyer could not appreciate the significance of the huge stove—not yet—but he now knew two false names assumed by Holmes: Cook and Hayes. Since several of the children's letters were written from Indianapolis, he headed there next.

In Indianapolis he had the assistance of Detective David Richards, and again they first inquired at the hotels near the Union Depot. The register of the Stubbins House had an entry for an Etta Pitsel, St. Louis, Missouri, arriving the twenty-fourth of September and leaving the twenty-eighth. The clerk recognized the photograph of Holmes as the man who had brought her to the hotel, and the photograph of Alice as "Etta." Moreover, on the morning of Friday, September 28, the clerk had received a telegram from Holmes, dated St. Louis, requesting him to bring Etta Pitsel to the depot to meet the St. Louis train for Cincinnati. This was the day Holmes left St. Louis with Nellie and Howard, telling their mother that he was going to take them to Indianapolis, where they would be cared for by a kind old lady.

It was now established that Holmes had left fifteen-year-old Alice in Indianapolis while he went to St. Louis to dispose of the check from the insurance company; that he left St. Louis on September 28 with Nellie and Howard Pitezel and picked up Alice in Indianapolis; and that the four of them were in Cincinnati for at least two nights, September 28 and 29.

Confident that Holmes had returned to Indianapolis from Cincinnati, Geyer spent more long hours checking hotel registers and again was rewarded. The Hotel English had a registry September 30 for three Canning children, Galva, Illinois. Since the children's grandparents' name was Canning and they lived in Galva, Geyer was certain he was on the right track. But after checking evey hotel and lodging house in Indianapolis, he could find no further record of the children. Then Detective Richards remembered that a small hotel known as the Circle House had gone out of business in the months since the children had disappeared. They obtained the register from a lawyer and found an entry for October 1 to October 6, again for three Canning children from Galva. The former proprietor, Mr. Herman Ackelow, was now running a saloon in West Indianapolis, and when questioned by the detectives he remembered that Holmes had told him Howard was a very bad boy, and that he was trying to place him in some institution or bind him out to some farmer, as he wanted to be rid of the responsibility of looking after this troublesome "nephew." Mr. Ackelow added that on a number of occasions his son went to the children's hotel room to call them for their meals and found them crying, evidently heartbroken and homesick.

From what Holmes had said about Howard, Detective Geyer was certain he had been murdered. But where? And when?

In Indianapolis, Holmes had also registered Miss Yoke at the Circle Park Hotel under the name of Mrs. Georgia Howard. She was there while Holmes was in Philadelphia with Howe and Alice for the purpose of identifying Pitezel's body. She returned September 30 and stayed until October 4, and her hotel was within one hundred feet of the Circle House, where Holmes had the children. She was almost within speaking distance of the children, yet she remained in total ignorance of their presence.

While at the Circle Park Hotel, Mrs. Georgia Howard had become intimate with the proprietress, a Mrs. Rodius. She informed her that her husband was a wealthy man, and that he owned real estate and cattle ranches in Texas. He also had considerable property in Berlin, Germany, she said, and they intended to go there as soon as he could get his business affairs in shape.

Geyer was reluctant to leave Indianapolis, as something told him Howard never left there alive, but he proceeded to Chicago. Mrs. Pitezel had told Geyer that the children's trunk was missing, and Holmes had said he left it at a hotel on West Madison Street in Chicago.

Assisted by Detective Sergeant John C. McGinn, Geyer made inquiries at every hotel within a mile of where Holmes said the children had stayed. Not a person remembered seeing them. Holmes had also claimed that his lawyer in Chicago, Wharton Plummer, had seen the children, but Plummer denied any such knowledge. Geyer even went to the "castle" on Sixty-third Street and talked to the janitor of the building, Pat Quinlan, a slim man about thirty-eight years old and with light, curly hair and a sandy moustache. Quinlan knew the Pitezel children very well, but had no knowledge of their whereabouts. He was convinced that if the Callowhill Street body was Pitezel, Holmes had murdered him and had subsequently murdered the children. If Holmes were to be hanged, he volunteered to spring the trap.

Holmes' most recent story, when he learned that Geyer would be making another search for the children, was that he had left them with a bricklayer named Edward Hatch, who had done odd chores around the Castle. Quinlan denounced Holmes as a dirty, lying scoundrel and said that Hatch was a decent, hardworking man who would not do anything wrong. But Hatch had moved and they could not locate him, so Geyer left the search for Hatch in the hands of Detective McGinn and went on to Detroit.

Matters became even more complicated in Detroit. Following the usual painstaking procedures, Geyer found that the girls had stayed one night at the New Western Hotel before moving into a boardinghouse at 91 Congress Street—where Alice had written a letter home. At neither place did the girls have a trunk. That missing trunk annoyed Geyer, for he knew it was with them in Indianapolis.

As for Holmes, he and Miss Yoke had spent the first night at the Hotel Normandie, then moved into a house at 54 Park Place.

The local Fidelity Mutual agent had turned up a lead that Geyer also explored. It was a real estate agent who had rented a house on the outskirts of town to Holmes—accompanied by a small boy, thus unsettling Geyer's hunch that Howard had never left Indianapolis. Getting permission to search it from the present occupants, Geyer found no evidence of holes dug in the floor of the basement or in the yard. There was a stove in the cellar, but the new occupant had noticed nothing unusual or improper about its contents when he moved in. He did remember, however, that a hole had been dug into one of the cellar walls, extending beneath the foundation for the back porch. It was an empty hole about four feet long, three feet wide, and three feet six inches deep.

Geyer remembered that Mrs. Pitezel had been in Detroit, too, and that she recalled staying at Geis' Hotel with Dessie and the baby. He checked with the housekeeper, and she remembered Mrs. Pitezel as never out of her room and apparently suffering from great mental anxiety.

The full tragedy of the movements in Detroit soon became apparent to Geyer as he reconstructed what had happened the previous October. Mrs. Pitezel, overwrought with fear and grief, was in her hotel room, warned by Holmes not to wander lest the detectives trace Ben through her movements. *A few blocks away,* Alice and Nellie played in their boardinghouse room, no doubt crying themselves to sleep out of homesickness. Yet Mrs. Pitezel thought the children were in Indianapolis, and they were writing letters to her in Galva, Illinois. In the şame city, meanwhile, were Holmes and Miss Yoke. Thinking herself to be Mrs. Howard, she assumed they were going from city to city so he could sell leases on his patent copier and get his business affairs in shape for their impending trip to Berlin. Not only was she unaware of the presence of Mrs. Pitezel and Dessie and the baby, on the one hand, or Alice and Nellie on the other—she was totally unaware even of their existence.

And Howard was nowhere to be seen.

Geyer wondered to himself what extraordinarily careful management—what evil genius—was necessary to have moved these three separate parties about the country, each of them ignorant of the others even though their paths would nearly cross. Holmes did it, however, and pulled it off successfully.

* * *

The intrepid detective headed next for Toronto, enlisting the help of an old friend on its police force, Detective Alf. Cuddy. Checking first with the hotels in the area of the Grand Trunk Depot, they traced Mrs. Pitezel to the Union House and Holmes to the Walker House, then later the Palmer House. Alice and Nellie had been registered at the Albion Hotel, and the clerk remembered that Holmes had come to check on them every day. Then, on the twenty-fifth of October, he paid their board bill and took the girls away with him.

Holmes' activities in the various cities had followed a regular pattern, and Geyer was certain he knew what happened next. "It is my impression," he wrote Philadelphia's Superintendent Linden, "that Holmes rented a house in Toronto the same as he did in Cincinnati, Ohio, and Detroit, Michigan, and that on the 25th of October he murdered the girls and disposed of their bodies by either burying them in the cellar, or some convenient place, or burning them in the heater. I intend to go to all the real estate agents and see if they can recollect having rented a house about the time to a man who only occupied it for a few days, and who represented that he wanted it for a widowed sister." Holmes had given this "widowed sister" story in Cincinnati and Detroit, and it was reasonable to assume he had used it here too.

After the first day of contacting real estate agents, Geyer and Cuddy realized just how immense this task was and how long it might take them to complete. Geyer decided to take the plunge and called in reporters. He told them the whole story of why he was in town and what he suspected had happened, and provided them with photographs of Holmes and the Pitezel family. The next morning every Toronto newspaper gave prominent mention to the story and asked good citizens with any information to contact Geyer or the police department.

Geyer's tactic worked. Now when they arrived at a real estate agent's office, there was no lengthy explanation to provide, no exhaustive check of the records—the agent had already done the checking. Then, on the day after the story broke in the newspapers, they returned to police headquarters in the evening to find a message that a man giving the name of Holmes had rented a house on the outskirts of the city—a house that stood in the middle of a field and was surrounded by a board fence six feet high. That had to be it.

Alas, it wasn't. When they explained their mission to the present occupants of the house, the man living there replied, "That accounts for that pile of loose dirt under the main building." They began to dig, and when it started to get dark they used coal-oil lamps so they could continue. But the pile of loose dirt yielded nothing. The next morning they checked with the agent who had rented the house and provided the lead. When he saw the photograph of Holmes, he said it was not the man who had rented his house.

Disappointed, Geyer began checking newspaper files for the names of private renters who had advertised their houses for rent during the period of Holmes' visit. As he was finishing this task, another report came to the police station—a man fitting Holmes' description had rented a house at 16 St. Vincent Street the past October, and for only one week. Geyer and Cuddy rushed to the house, but instead of going to number 16, they called at number 18 to talk to the neighbor, an old Scotchman named Thomas William Ryves. He was the one who had seen the newspaper stories and called the police. Mr. Ryves positively identified Alice as one of the girls, but said he never got a good look at Nellie, and he wasn't positively sure the man was Holmes. He recalled that the man had borrowed a spade, as he wanted to arrange a place in his cellar for keeping potatoes, and that the only furniture brought to the house was an old bed, a mattress, and a big trunk. The trunk was later removed, but the bed and mattress stayed there.

The two detectives asked Ryves to meet them at the house in an hour. They hurried to the home of Mrs. Frank Nudel, who owned and rented the house on St. Vincent Street. She and her daughter immediately recognized the photograph of Holmes. This seemed too good to be true, and they rushed back to the house, where Ryves was anxiously awaiting their return. They asked if he could find them a shovel, and he brought one out of his house—the same one he had loaned to Holmes.

After they had explained why they were there, the lady occupying the house consented to let them inspect the cellar. It was small and dark, just ten feet square and not more than four and a half feet in depth, forcing them to work by lamps.

Detective Geyer later disclosed what happened: "Taking the spade and pushing it into the earth, so as to determine whether it had been lately dug up, we finally discovered a soft spot in the southwest corner. Forcing the spade into the earth, we found it

No. 16 St. Vincent St., Toronto, Canada, where Holmes murdered Alice and Nellie Pitezel.

easy digging, and after going about one foot, a horrible stench arose. This convinced us that we were on the right spot, and our coats were thrown off, and with renewed confidence, we continued our digging. The deeper we dug, the more horrible the odor became, and when we reached the depth of three feet, we discovered what appeared to be the bone of the forearm of a human being."

They threw some dirt in the hole, to keep the stench down, and called Inspector Stark of the police department. He told them to make arrangements with B. D. Humphrey, an undertaker, who would assist them in the exhumation of the bodies. Geyer suggested to the undertaker that he take several pairs of rubber gloves along, as the bodies were in such a state of putrefaction it would be impossible to lift them out of the hole without them. Back to the cellar they went, with Humphrey now assisting them, and in a short time they unearthed the remains of the two little

1.—The children now realized their predicament and began to beg piteously for mercy.

2.—Holmes arranged a rubber hose to the gas jet and put the end of the same through the hole into the trunk and turned on the gas.

girls, Alice and Nellie Pitezel. A messenger was dispatched to Humphrey's undertaking establishment to bring back two coffins. When they arrived, the coffins were brought into the kitchen, and they proceeded to lift the remains out of the hole.

"Alice was found lying on her side," Geyer recalled, "with her hand to the west. Nellie was found lying on her face, with her head to the south, her plaited hair hanging neatly down her back. . . . As Nellie's limbs were found resting on Alice's, we first began with her. We lifted her as gently as possible, but owing to the decomposed state of the body, the weight of her plaited hair hanging down her back, pulled the scalp from off her head. A sheet had been spread in which to lay the remains, and after we succeeded in getting it out of the hole, it was placed in the sheet, taken upstairs, and deposited in the coffin.

"Again we returned to the cellar," he continued, "and gently lifting what remained of poor Alice, we placed her in another sheet, took her upstairs, and placed her in a coffin by the side of her sister. . . . By this time Toronto was wild with excitement. The news had spread to every part of the city. The St. Vincent Street house was besieged with newspaper men, sketch artists, and others. Everybody seemed to be pleased with our success, and congratulations, mingled with expressions of horror over the discovery were heard everywhere."

Detective Geyer telegraphed the authorities in Philadelphia, and recorded that "thus it was proved that little children cannot be murdered in this day and generation, beyond the possibility of discovery."

* * *

Geyer rested for a day and then resumed his task. Personal identification might be difficult, since the bodies were badly decomposed, so he sought other evidence. He talked to the people who had occupied the house right after Holmes. Their boy had found a toy in a closet—a little wooden egg with a snake inside that would spring out when the egg was opened in the middle. Just such a toy was on a list of playthings the children had with them.

Another link was provided by one of the women who lived in

the house after Holmes. The Pitezel girls had been buried naked, with just part of a waistpiece and what appeared to be part of a ribbon with them in their cellar grave. This woman had noticed some rags and straw hanging from a chimney, and they turned out to be part of some children's clothes that had been partially burned. The straw had been lit, but the clothing had been shoved into the chimney too tightly and had not been completely destroyed. The woman found part of a striped waist of a grayish color, a piece of woolen garment of brownish red, and part of a dress of bluish color; and in the woodbox were a pair of girls' button boots, an odd boot, and other parts of the clothing of a female. She had thrown all of this away, but they answered Mrs. Pitezel's description of the clothing worn by her missing daughters.

The doctors' examination of the bodies indicated that death probably had been caused by suffocation. Geyer and Cuddy suggested that Holmes may have placed the girls in a trunk after drugging them with chloroform, and then applied gas through an opening in the trunk until they were dead. While this was just a theory, there was one piece of evidence that gave rise to the thought—the trunk police seized at the time of Holmes' arrest in Boston. It was believed to be the same trunk he had used throughout the trip, and in it had been drilled a hole exactly the size of an ordinary gas tube's diameter.

The undertaker also reported that both of Nellie's feet were missing. At first it was supposed they had been struck by a shovel while digging and cut off in that way, but a search of the cellar failed to reveal them and it was then thought they were amputated by Holmes for some reason. The undertaker later changed his mind, and suggested that perhaps the bones had crumbled and were in the coffin with the body. It was not clear why this should be a mystery since the bodies were not so totally decomposed that the bones had disintegrated.

Geyer now braced himself for the necessity of bringing Mrs. Pitezel to Toronto to identify the bodies and testify at the coroner's inquest. She left from Chicago, where newspaper reporters interviewed her on boarding the train and wired her scheduled arrival to the Toronto papers. A crowd, largely of the rougher element, was waiting for her, and Geyer had to push through it to rescue her from their curiosity as fast as possible. He placed her in a carriage and took her to the Rossin House, where he was staying. He had made arrangements for her to be placed in a room opposite his own and to be left undisturbed.

Mrs. Pitezel reached her room in an absolutely prostrated condition. Restoratives were applied, and she asked the detective, amid her tears and moans, "Oh, Mr. Geyer, is it true that you have found Alice and Nellie buried in a cellar?" He did all he could to calm her, and told her to prepare for the worst. She said she would try and bear up with it and do the best she could. Geyer then told her as gently as possible that he had found the girls, but he did not describe to her their horrible condition nor under what circumstances they were discovered. Several ladies from the hotel continued to watch over Mrs. Pitezel throughout the day.

After a fitful night's sleep, Mrs. Pitezel prepared herself for the ordeal of identifying the bodies. Geyer and Cuddy assisted her into the carriage, taking along a supply of brandy and smelling salts. At the deadhouse he checked to see that everything was ready before bringing her in.

"I found," he said, "that Coroner Johnston, Dr. Caven and several of his assistants, had removed the putrid flesh from the skull of Alice; the teeth had been nicely cleaned and the bodies covered with canvas. The head of Alice was covered with paper, and a hole sufficiently large had been cut in it, so that Mrs. Pitezel could see the teeth. The hair of both children had been carefully washed and laid on the canvas sheet which was covering Alice. Coroner Johnston said that we could now bring Mrs. Pitezel in. I entered the waiting room and told her we were ready, and with Cuddy on one side of her, and I on the other, we entered and led her up to the slab, upon which was lying all that remained of poor Alice. In an instant she recognized the teeth and hair as that of her daughter, Alice. Then turning around to me she said, 'Where is Nellie?' About this time she noticed the long black plait of hair belonging to Nellie lying in the canvas. She could stand it no longer, and the shrieks of that poor forlorn creature are still ringing in my ears. Tears were trickling down the cheeks of strong men who stood about us. The sufferings of the stricken mother were beyond description. We gently led her out of the room, and into the carriage. She returned to the Rossin House completely overcome with grief and despair, and had one fainting spell after another. The ladies in the hotel visited her in her room and spoke kindly to her, and expressed their sympathy with her in her sad bereavement and this seemed in a measure to ease her mind."

Her ordeal was not over, however, for that afternoon she had to testify at the inquest. For two and a half hours she told her story, becoming so weak at times that her voice was inaudible and they feared she would collapse. When she was finished, she returned to the matron's room and had scarcely entered it when she became hysterical. Several doctors present at the inquest had to work on her for an hour before she was in any condition to return to the hotel.

The remains of the two girls were buried in St. James' cemetery, the expenses being borne by the Toronto authorities. Detective Geyer and Mrs. Pitezel took a train to Detroit, where he got off. She continued on to Chicago, where she was placed in the care of the women of the Christian Endeavor Society until she was able to return to her parents in Galva.

*　*　*

Geyer now confronted the remainder of his task: to find out what had happened to the boy, Howard. He checked again with the real estate people in Detroit who had reported seeing a boy with Holmes. Upon closer questioning they now said there were several persons with children in the office at the same time, and they *thought*, but were not certain, that one of the children, a small boy, was with Holmes.

Geyer again searched the house on the outskirts of town, where he had found an empty cellar hole about four feet long, three feet wide, and three feet six inches deep. Still no evidence of Howard was produced.

Alice had written her grandparents from Detroit, and in that letter she stated simply that "Howard is not with us now"—no mention of where they became separated. She also complained of the cold and asked her grandparents to "Tell mamma that I have to have a coat. I nearly freeze in that thin jacket. We have to stay in all the time." Of course, Holmes would not buy coats for the girls. It would be a waste of money since he intended to kill them soon, and by forcing them to stay in their hotel room he avoided the risk of a chance encounter with their mother, who was within a ten-minute walk of their hotel.

Suppose the hole in the Detroit cellar was intended for the girls—a reasonable assumption considering what had been discovered in Toronto—and Holmes had to leave before he could complete his morbid task. If Howard was not separated from the girls in Detroit—and there was now no hard evidence that he ever made it to that city—then he must have been separated at some earlier point in the journey. Geyer headed back to Indianapolis.

With the assistance, again, of Detective David Richards, Geyer began checking with every real estate agent in the Indianapolis area, searching for a house that had been rented early in October 1894 to a man who wanted it for a widowed sister and who occupied it but a short time.

Meanwhile, Special Assistant District Attorney Barlow had been studying the letters from the Pitezel children and he wrote Geyer about some of his observations. An analysis of their text, he said, convinced him that the girls wrote these letters from Indianapolis on October 6, 7, and 8. The first one, written by Nellie, was dated October 6—a Saturday. The second letter, written by Alice, was also dated the sixth, but it evidently was written on the following day and should have been dated the seventh. "Alice's eyes hurts," writes Nellie on Saturday, "so she won't write this time." "I have read so much in Uncle Tom's book," writes Alice, "that I could not see to write yesterday when Nell and Howard did." Moreover, Alice expects "this Sunday to pass away slower than I don't know what." And then the third letter, also written by Alice, is simply dated "Monday morning" without a date affixed, and she speaks of having written two or three letters to her mother and promises, "I will send this with my letter I wrote yesterday and didn't send off."

The significance of these dates was that the children had apparently stayed at the same hotel—the Circle House—at least until Monday, October 8. Yet the register had shown them leaving on the sixth. Geyer talked again to Mr. Ackelow, the hotel proprietor turned bartender, and he checked the hotel register again, this time more carefully. The hotel's books had been very carelessly kept, and Geyer now discovered that the last payment of their board was on October 10, after which they left. Since he knew for a certainty that the girls had arrived in Detroit on the evening of October 12, that left only forty-eight hours to be accounted for. Howard had disappeared during that time, and either in Indianapolis or between that city and Detroit.

Alice's Monday morning letter was of significance, too, in its telling of Howard's alleged misbehavior. "One morning Mr. H. told me to tell him to stay in the next morning, *that he wanted him and would come and get him and take him out* and I told him and he would not stay in at all, he was out when he came." This was precisely what Holmes did at the Albion Hotel in Toronto: He called for the girls and took them out on the morning of October 25, and they never returned. Poor Howard, if he had known the fate that was in store for him, would have continued to stay out "when he came."

Barlow produced a further clue. After the Fidelity Mutual Insurance Association paid the claim on Pitezel's policy, it received a letter from Alice thanking them for the prompt payment. It had been mailed on October 11, and was postmarked "Chic. Richmond & Cin. R.P.O."—a government postal route between Chicago, Indianapolis, Cincinnati, and Detroit. It appeared reasonably certain, therefore, that the girls were on a train somewhere between these cities on October 11.

Detective Geyer was recalled to Philadelphia for a few days' rest and consultation. He was told that Holmes, faced with the discovery of the bodies in Toronto, remained silent for more than two hours while District Attorney Graham and his assistants showered him with questions. Graham had hoped to take Holmes by surprise with the news of the discovery, and extract, if possible, a confession. Word of Graham's plans reached the prison keepers too late, however, and the guard who went to Holmes' cell found him looking over the newspaper dispatches with an air which, if not for real, was certainly a marvelous assumption of coolness. The insurance company was now more determined than ever to discover what had happened to Howard, and they assigned their chief inspector, W. E. Gary, to join Geyer in the search.

Geyer and Gary followed up on leads in Chicago, Logansport and Peru, Indiana, Montpelier Junction, Ohio, and Adrian, Michigan—all without success. Back in Indianapolis, they checked out every house that had been listed for rent in October. No less than nine hundred supposed clues were run out. Then they began with a search of the small towns just beyond the city of Indianapolis. Detective Geyer wrote Philadelphia's Superintendent of Police Linden, "By Monday we will have searched every outlying town, except Irvington, and another day will conclude that. After Irvington, I scarcely know where we shall go."

Weary and discouraged, the two detectives took a trolley to Irvington the following Tuesday and walked into the first real estate office they saw. Geyer opened up the package of papers and photographs he had untied and tied over a thousand times, until it had become soiled and ragged from wear. He asked the pleasant old gentleman who greeted them if he knew of a house in his town that had been rented for a short time in October by a man who said he wanted it for a widowed sister. He then handed him the photograph of Holmes. The man, a Mr. Brown, listened, and then adjusting his glasses took a long look at the photograph.

"Yes," he said, "I remember a man who rented a house under such circumstances in October of 1894, and this picture looks like him very much. I did not have the renting of the house, but I had the keys, and one day last fall, this man came into my office and in a very abrupt way said, I want the keys for that house. I remember the man very well, because I did not like his manner, and I felt that he should have had more respect for my gray hairs."

While Mr. Brown was talking, Geyer and Gary stood still. When he had finished, they looked at each other and sat down. All the toil, all the weary days and weeks of travel in the hottest months of the year, alternating between faith and hope and discouragement and despair—all were recompensed in that one moment when they saw the veil about to lift.

*   *   *

77

Dr. Thompson, the owner of the Irvington house, identified the photograph of Holmes as the man he rented it to in October. A boy in his employ, Elvet Moorman, identified both Holmes and Howard. On arriving at the house, Geyer found it to be a one-and-a-half-story cottage, standing in a secluded place apart from any other houses.

They searched the cellar first, but the floor showed no signs of disturbance. The outside of the house was scrutinized next, and Geyer found a portion of a trunk, which he retained as evidence. Then the detectives turned their attention to the barn and outhouses. In the barn was a large coal stove, about three and a half feet high and twenty-two inches in diameter. On its top Geyer found what appeared to be bloodstains. Wherever a soft spot was discovered in the earth, they dug deeply, but they found no body.

Cottage at Irvington, Indiana, where Holmes murdered Howard Pitezel.

By this time, word had spread and several hundred people had gathered around the house. It was getting late, so Geyer and Gary checked with the agent who had rented the house, and he too confirmed that it had been rented by Holmes.

At the telegraph office in Indianapolis, Geyer wired Mrs. Pitezel, asking, "Did missing trunk have a strip of blue calico, white figure over seam on the bottom." Her reply came back in the affirmative. The missing trunk had been found.

While he was at the telegraph office, Geyer received a telephone call from the city editor of the Indianapolis *Evening News*. He was told to wait for the arrival of Dr. Thompson, the owner of the house, and his partner Dr. J. F. Barnhill—that they had something important to show him. The two doctors arrived in a few minutes and opened a small package containing several pieces of charred bone, which they declared were the femur and skull of a child between eight and twelve years old. Dr. Barnhill then explained that after the detectives had left, he and Dr. Thompson had continued the search. They were accompanied by two boys, Walter Jenny and Oscar Kettenbach, who decided to play detective too and went into the cellar. A chimney led from the basement to the roof of the house, and in the chimney was a pipe hole about three and a half feet from the floor. Young Walter had put his arm in the opening and pulled out a handful of ashes, among which was one of the pieces of bone. The boys continued to bring out ashes and pieces of bone and then ran and called the doctors.

The detectives and the doctors rushed back to Irvington, where they found the entire neighborhood assembled at the house. The police marshall cleared people from the house, leaving only the detectives and doctors and several members of the press. With a hammer and chisel, Geyer took down the lower part of the chimney. He then took an old fly screen that he found in the house and, using it as a sieve, let the ashes and soot fall from the chimney. In it was an almost complete set of teeth and a piece of the jaw. At the bottom of the chimney was a large charred mass, which upon being cut disclosed a portion of the stomach, liver, and spleen, baked quite hard. The pelvis of the body was also found, and all this was handed to Dr. Barnhill for examination.

In the chimney Geyer also found some of the iron fastenings that belonged to the trunk, some buttons, a small scarfpin, and a crochet needle. The bottom of the stove yielded a substance that they supposed was formed by blood and grease from the body. Later, searching for outside evidence, Geyer found a boy's coat in possession of a grocer in Irvington. The grocer said that in October a man called at his store and left the coat, saying that a boy would call for it the next morning, but that the boy never came.

Poor Mrs. Pitezel was called upon once again to leave her parents' home in Galva, Illinois, and testify at a coroner's inquest. She had hoped to the end that her son had been placed in some institution or bound out to a farmer, as Holmes had threatened in his conversation with the Indianapolis hotel proprietor.

She identified the overcoat found at the grocer's as Howard's. The trunk was easily recognized, because of a strip of calico her father had pasted along the bottom. Ben had bought his son a little spinning top and a tin man at the world's fair, and these were found in the house by Geyer. She also identified a scarfpin and a pair of shoes as Howard's and the crochet needle as Alice's. All of these had been found in the Irvington house.

Elvet Moorman, the boy who ran errands for Dr. Thompson, testified that he went to the house one afternoon and saw furniture being unloaded from a transfer wagon, with Holmes and Howard helping out. Later in the afternoon he returned to milk a cow that was kept in the barn, and while he was milking, Holmes asked him to assist him in putting up a stove, which he did. Elvet asked why he did not make a connection for natural gas and use a gas stove, and Holmes replied that he did not think gas was healthy for children. Elvet said that Howard was present when the stove was set up, and that after the two disappeared, he had examined the house and found a lot of corn rubbish on the floor that seemed to indicate that a fire had been made with corncobs.

The two doctors and a dentist, Dr. Byram, testified regarding the remains, and an Indianapolis repairman named Albert Schiffling told how Holmes and Howard came into his shop on October 3 with two cases of surgical instruments that Holmes

Holmes held the boy between his knees, and wrapped his fingers about his throat, slowly closing them upon it like a vise.

wanted sharpened. He returned for the instruments on October 8, paid for the repairs, and took them away.

The coroner's jury had no difficulty in finding that Howard Pitezel had come to his death at the hands of H. H. Holmes.

6

HOLMES CASTLE REVEALS HORRORS

Queer Tank Discovered,
Along with Vats of Quicklime,
Skeletons, and Charred Bones;
Proof that Bodies were Cremated
in Englewood.

FOUL GAS TAKES FIRE

Explosion Disturbs the Searchers
in the Castle's Basement.

MORE CRIMES ADDED

Common Fates Awaited
Mrs. Conner and Daughter, Miss
Emeline Cigrand, and Williams Sisters.

HOW MANY VICTIMS?

When the bodies of Alice and Nellie Pitezel were found on July 15, the world began to view Holmes in a new light. Previously he was seen as a master swindler, almost charming in his audacity, who may have had a falling-out with his accomplice and killed him. Now it was established that he was a cold-blooded killer who did not hesitate to murder two young girls in a horrible manner. Rumors had circulated for months about the possibility of other murders, particularly of the typewriter Minnie Williams and her sister. Now those rumors seemed much more plausible.

Chicago, as Holmes' base of operations, became obsessed with speculation about the monstrous activities that were supposed to have taken place in the Holmes "castle" on Sixty-third Street. The police decided to investigate, using as their excuse that they were searching for clues to the disappearance of the Williams sisters. Detective Sergeants Fitzpatrick and Norton, accompanied by Pinkerton operative Frank Wind, led the search, and what they discovered within the Castle's walls made the most fertile imagination seem tame in comparison.

The first floor produced nothing unusual—it consisted mostly of the shops that faced onto Sixty-third and Wallace streets. The third floor contained Holmes' private office on the Sixty-third Street side and otherwise held the rooms he had built as a world's fair hotel. It was the second floor and the basement that most interested the police and the public.

A labyrinth of blind hallways, secret passages, and concealed rooms and trapdoors awaited to confuse and snare any uninvited visitor to the second floor. Holmes kept another suite of rooms

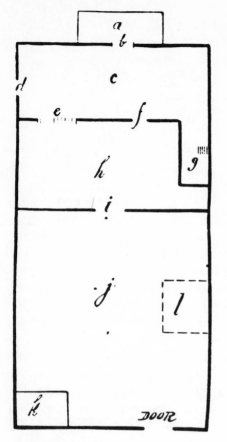

Basement of Holmes' Castle, Sixty-Third and Wallace Streets. A—Gas tank under alleyway. B—Entrance to same concealed by brick wall destroyed by the police. C—South end of basement. D—Window and door under sidewalk. E—Stairway from rear. F—Entrance to center of basement. G—Secret chamber, with stairway on west side, concealed by manure and dirt and opened by police. Where woman's shoe was found four feet underground. H—Center of basement. I—Entrance to north end of basement. J—North end of basement. K—Coal bin underneath which a shirt and drawers were found. L—bottom of elevator shaft, reached by concealed stairs and a false trap door in bathroom on second floor. From the *Chicago Times-Herald*, July 25, 1895, p. 2. Courtesy of the Illinois State Historical Library.

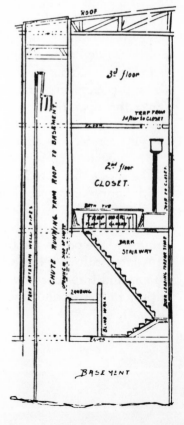

Sectional view showing the means Holmes had of secretly getting to street or basement. From the *Chicago Times-Herald*, July 25, 1895, p. 2. Courtesy of the Illinois State Historical Library.

facing Sixty-third Street as his personal apartment. Besides those quarters, in Herbert Asbury's vivid account, "the second floor contained thirty-five rooms. Half a dozen were fitted up as ordinary sleeping-chambers, and there were indications that they had been occupied by the various women who had worked for the monster, or to whom he had made love while awaiting an opportunity to kill them. Several of the other rooms were without windows, and could be made air-tight by closing the doors. One was completely filled by a huge safe, almost large enough for a bank vault, into which a gas-pipe had been introduced. Another was lined with sheet iron covered by asbestos, and showed traces of fire. Some had been sound-proofed, while others had extremely low ceilings, and trapdoors in the floors from which ladders led to smaller rooms beneath. In all of the rooms on the second floor, as well as in the great safe, were gas-pipes with cut-off valves in plain sight. But these valves were fakes; the flow of gas was actually controlled by a series of cut-offs concealed in the closet of Holmes' bedroom. Apparently one of his favorite methods of murder was to lock a victim in one of the rooms and then turn on the gas; and the police believed that in the asbestos-lined chamber he had devised a means of introducing fire, so that the gas-pipe became a terrible blow-torch from which there was no escape. Also in Holmes' closet was an electric bell which rang whenever a door was opened anywhere on the second floor."

In Holmes' office was a huge stove, six feet high and several feet in diameter. Part of a bone was found in the contents of the ash-pan, and another bone, resembling a rib, was picked out of the grate. A woman's slipper, badly scorched, and a piece of a dress were also found in the ashes. After the police left for another part of the Castle, reporters dismantled the stovepipe and examined the chimney. Clinging to the brickwork was a bunch of human hair, long and evidently a woman's. Apparently the hair had been in the stove and had been pulled into the chimney by a strong draft.

A bankbook found in Holmes' office belonged to a Lucy Burbank and recorded her deposits in the First National Bank. They were substantial, with Miss Burbank putting money in the bank nearly every day and sometimes as much as $300. But nobody knew who Lucy Burbank was.

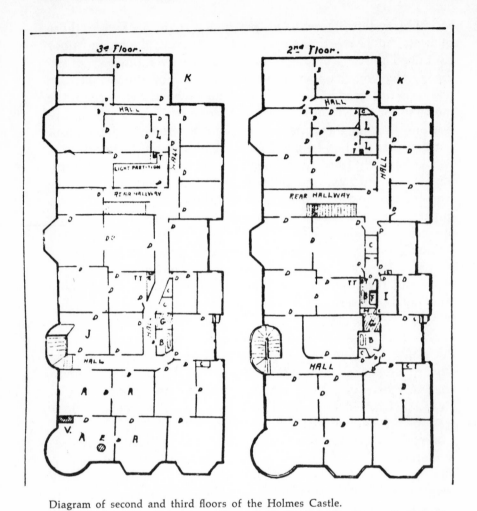

Diagram of second and third floors of the Holmes Castle.
A—Rooms used by Holmes as offices. B—Bathrooms. D—Doors. E—Stove in which Holmes is supposed to have burned his victims. F—Trap door in floor of bathroom or closet opening into secret stairway, where Holmes could escape to the street or basement through chute. C—Closets. I—Laboratories. J—Miss Williams' room. K—Alleyway. V—False vaults. G—Chute running from roof to basement. H—Blind wall and landing between secret stairway and chute. Over this landing is a secret hiding place with access only through the top of closet off from dark room I. T—Trap leading from third floor into laboratory on second. TT—Trap leading from third floor into bathroom on second. From *Chicago Times-Herald*, July 26, 1895, p. 2. Courtesy of the Illinois State Historical Library.

Where the explosion took place—the gas tank in the basement. From the *Chicago Times-Herald*, July 21, 1895, p. 2. Courtesy of the Illinois State Historical Library.

The searchers working by electric light.

Where the bones were found.

From the *Chicago Daily Tribune*, July 25, 1895, p. 2.

In one of the sleeping rooms on the second floor, police found bloodstained overalls and a bloodstained undershirt. Microscopic examination also revealed bloodstains on the floor and walls of the room, leading to the bathroom adjacent to it. In this bathroom was a hidden trapdoor that led down secret stairs to the basement; adjoining it was a dummy elevator that led from the third floor to the basement—a shaft large enough to accommodate a body. More stains, all of which proved to be of human blood, were found in the bathroom and down the stairway.

Trap door on the second floor.

Vault and quicklime grave.

Castle stove that furnished clues.

Holmes' private laboratory.

From the *Chicago Daily Tribune*, July 26, 1895, p. 2. Courtesy of the Illinois State Historical Library

In still another room, wedged into the plastering where a doorsill had been torn away, were a woolen shirt, a little girl's dress, and a pair of shoes. They had been embedded so long that the fabric scarcely held together.

It was the basement, however, that bared the most chilling evidence of maniacal homicide. Scattered about and buried at various points were piles of bones that later proved to be human, with chicken bones and other animal bones mixed in among them, perhaps for the very purpose of confusing the evidence should they ever be discovered. More bones were carefully sifted out of pits of lime. Dr. C. P. Stringfield, one of the doctors working with the police, found the ribs and pelvis bones of a child, from eight to fourteen years old, among them. Buried in quicklime as they were, he estimated they had reached their present state of decomposition in a period of six months to two years.

A barrel with extra heavy hoops was discovered to contain acid, and in a corner of the basement was a dissecting table, with a box of surgical knives. Under this table were a number of women's skeletons, and one of the theories that gained currency was that Holmes sometimes separated the flesh of his victims from their bones and sold the skeletons to medical schools. A storeroom revealed a bloody noose and a workbench stained with blood. Buried beneath the floor were two brick vaults, each about six feet long and three feet wide, filled with quicklime.

Also scattered about the basement were several strange machines, including one that resembled a medieval torture rack. Holmes had a theory, it was said, that the human body could be stretched to twice its normal length, thus creating a race of giants. Perhaps this was the "elasticity determinator" with which he tested that theory.

As police and workmen continued to explore the basement, a great surprise awaited them, and the exact nature and sequence of the events that followed depended on the newspaper you read. The New York *World* reported that "they encountered a wall that gave forth a hollow sound. As soon as this wall was broken through a horrible smell was encountered and fumes like those of a charnel house rushed forth. A plumber was sent for, and the workmen gathered about while he proceeded to investigate. The

DETECTIVE SERGEANT FITZPATRICK.
From the *Chicago Times-Herald*,
July 25, 1895, p. 2. Courtesy of the
Illinois State Historical Library.

PAT QUINLAN, the janitor.
From the Chicago *Times-Herald*,
July 25, 1895, p. 2. Courtesy of the
Illinois State Historical Society.

first thing the plumber did was to light a match. Then there was a terrific explosion that shook the building, while flames poured forth into the cellar. The plumber was the only man who escaped uninjured, and an ambulance took the other workmen to the hospital. Then a thorough search of this mysterious chamber was made by the police. They found that the brick wall had concealed a tank curiously constructed. This tank had contained an oil whose fumes, the chemists say, would destroy human life within less than a minute. There were evidences about the cellar of this mysterious and deadly oil having been used. . . . . A small box was found in the center of the tank. When this was opened by Fire Marshall James Kenyon an evil-smelling vapor rushed out. All ran except Kenyon, who was overpowered by the stench. He was dragged out and carried upstairs, and for two hours acted like one demented."

The Chicago *Inter Ocean*, on the other hand, reported that "Chief Kenyon was first out, and he had no sooner reached the ground than he became half delirious from the gas and started down the alley. Several of his men followed him, while the bystanders and the police, rushing to the top of the narrow tank hole, pulled out the firemen, who were now plainly under the influence of the gas. They recovered as soon as they reached the air, but not so the chief. He was pursued for a block and was finally caught and taken to a drug store almost unconscious. There Dr. Meek was called in, and soon after Chief Kenyon was able to resume work."

What the men had encountered was actually a double tank. The outer one was of cedar construction, cylindrical in shape, ten feet long and six feet in diameter, with numerous pipes running in various directions. Inside it was a zinc tank that contained the gas. When it was overturned by the firemen, the fluid in it mixed with a black deposit at the bottom of the cedar tank, a cloud of bluish vapor arose, and the men were overcome by the fumes.

The mystery of the double tank was explained, at least tentatively, by Clarence A. Phillips, who was now in the grocery business but said he built the tank for Holmes in 1890. Holmes told him it was for the purpose of holding crude oil used in bending plate glass. Phillips did not know how the oil was to be used, but he later learned that Holmes abandoned that particular scheme after breaking forty dollars' worth of plate glass, but not before he had swindled a number of persons who bought stock in the "Warner Glass Bending Company." Later Holmes told Phillips he was using the tank to hold a mixture of gasoline and certain chemicals by which he produced illuminating gas—the contrivance that got him in trouble with the city gas company.

The tank probably was constructed to aid Holmes in those schemes, but evidence developed to show that he later found another—and far more sinister—use for the tank. The *Inter Ocean* obtained a statement from a man who worked on it, withholding his name at his request because he was a member of one of the best-known firms in the city, a firm that manufactured large oil-burning furnaces and applied oil burners to other furnaces.

DETECTIVE SERGEANT NORTON. From the *Chicago Times-Herald*, July 25, 1895, p. 2. Courtesy of the Illinois State Historical Library.

"In April 1890," he stated, "H. H. Holmes came to us and said that he wanted a thoroughtly competant [sic] man to adjust an

93

oil burner to a furnace. As he seemed to consider the work of unusual importance I decided to attend to it personally."

The anonymous but obviously knowledgeable source continued his story:

"Holmes explained to me that he built the furnace himself, and had made an oil burner, but that it was not a success, that he could not obtain with it the necessary amount of heat. I told him that in order to make a satisfactory burner it was necessary for me to understand the construction of the furnace. At first he was adverse [sic] to showing it to me but when I told him that unless he did I could not guarantee to satisfy him, he showed it to me. I found that the furnace contained an inner chamber of fire brick. This was about three feet high, the same in width, and eight or nine feet long. The furnace was so constructed that the flames did not penetrate this chamber, but surrounded it. Two slight openings were left in the top of it, through which any gas forming could escape from the inner chamber. It would of course be consumed in the fire. In fact, the general plan of the furnace was not unlike that of a crematory for dead bodies, and with the provision already described there would be absolutely no odor from the furnace.

"I put in a burner which used oil from the tank in the alley. It was a success, for the furnace could be heated to a temperature of 3,000 degrees. . . . Holmes explained to me that he would use the big furnace in bending plate glass. The dimensions of the inner chamber were not large enough to admit a very large piece of glass, but at the time this fact did not impress me.

"It is my opinion," added the furnace agent, "that Holmes really did plan the furnace originally for his scheme of bending plate glass, and that the idea of using it to destroy human bodies came to him after he killed his first victim in the building. A dumb elevator ran from his office to the basement, and nothing would be easier than to lower a body by it to the basement and shove it into the furnace, in which there was ample room for it and in which it would be consumed in a very brief time, leaving only a handful of ashes. The gases arising from combustion would escape through the small vents in the inner chamber and be consumed in the intense flames of the furnace. Any trace of the odor that might remain would be carried up the small chimney leading through the roof and be carried off in the atmosphere."

If this plan was indeed adopted by Holmes, it was the surest one that could be devised. Holmes would be the first to realize the value of a crematory as a destroyer of evidence. And since the furnace had been removed some time before the police investigation, by order of a building inspector who considered it a fire hazard inappropriate for a residential and office building, any ashes it may have contained had now disappeared as well.

But how could Holmes have kept the world ignorant of these peculiarities of his Castle for so long? Rumors had been plentiful, but nobody had suggested anything as bizarre as what the police investigation revealed. The answer seems to be that he changed workmen so quickly and persistently that none of them saw but a fragment of the Castle—apparently no worker who began constructing a room would finish it, for Holmes would find some excuse to fire him or transfer him to another area. Undoubtedly this often served a secondary purpose, too, for Holmes could claim poor workmanship as his excuse for firing someone and could seek to avoid paying him for that reason.

Even with such frantic precautions, workmen would get together and place bits of stories together and Holmes himself would prove indiscreet. Bricklayer George Bowman, for example, helped build the vault and told why the job was suddenly transferred to an employee who was more trusted.

"I don't know what to make of Holmes," pondered Bowman, "but I think when you say he was crazy on the subject of life insurance and the murder of people you are not putting the case half strong enough. Why, I hadn't been working for him but two days before he came around and asked me if I didn't think it pretty hard work, this bricklaying. He asked me if I wouldn't like to make money easier than that, and of course I told him yes. A few days after he came over to me and, pointing down to the basement, said, 'You see that man down there? Well, that's my brother-in-law, and he has got no love for me, neither have I for him. Now, it would be the easiest matter for you to drop a stone on that fellow's head while you're at work and I will give you $50 if you do.' I was so badly scared I didn't know what to say or do, but I didn't drop the stone and got out of the place soon after. I didn't see the man Holmes represented to be his brother-in-law, nor did I ever learn his name. The incident was one I couldn't forget for a long time, for the diabolical proposition was made in about the same manner one would expect from a friend who was asking you the most trivial question."

Bowman added that near the house was a high sidewalk under which Holmes frequently dug holes in which he mysteriously buried stuff. He thought an excavation under the sidewalk might disclose something.

Not only was the building oddly constructed, it was poorly constructed as well. The false fronts projected by Holmes in his personal and business affairs were matched by the false battlements of his Castle, and both gave evidence that Holmes was one inclined to put the best he had on the outside.

The street fronts of his building were constructed to impress people, and the corner drug store, in particular, was a beautiful piece of work. A semihexagon entrance bowed in at one corner, and in the center of the entrance was a massive pillar topped with an elaborate and elegant composite capital, radiant with harmonious colors, which supported an open column of curved glass windows towering high above. The ceiling of the entrance was graced with a beautiful design representing a Catherine wheel, arranged about the supporting capital in such a manner as to dazzle the eyes of anyone who might attempt to study its pattern.

The interior of the drug store was decorated with frescoed stucco work, delightfully arranged in mild colors, and the floor was laid with alternative black and white diamond-shaped tiling. Immediately back of the store was a winding staircase that led from the outside to the top of the Castle. This stairway was enclosed in what appeared to be a grand oriel window projecting from the outside wall and supported from about midway between the ground and the first floor by a corbel of honeycomb design.

Elsewhere, however, this was the situation found by the building inspector who was called in while police were making their investigation:

DEPARTMENT OF BUILDINGS

Joseph Downey, Commissioner

Chicago, July 23d, 1895

Special report on H. H. Holmes' Building, S.W. Corner 63rd and Wallace streets:

Size of building, 50 x 125 feet, three-story and basement; stores and flats, five stores, two facing 63rd Street, and three on Wallace Street.

The structural parts of inside are all weak and dangerous. Built of the poorest and cheapest kind of material. A combination bay window and winding stairway on Wallace Street side, starting at second story joist and projecting three feet from building line, is breaking away from the building and is dangerous.

All dividing partitions between flats are combustible. Building was built in sections, and several parts weakened by fire, and not properly repaired. There is an uneven settlement of foundations, in some places as much as four inches in a span of 20 feet. The temporary roof put up after fire in the building is not properly constructed. The secret stairway and trap door leading from the bathroom and also underground gas tank does not interfere with the construction of the building. The stores are the only habitable parts of the building. The rest of the building should be condemned. The sanitary condition of the building is horrible.

Respectfully submitted,

E. F. LAUGHLIN,

Inspector.

On August 19, shortly after the police completed their investigation of its chambers, the Holmes Castle was destroyed by a fire of mysterious origins. Any remaining secrets would stay safely buried in the rubble, but enough had already been discovered to connect H. H. Holmes to a chain of ghastly murders within its walls.

* * *

Perhaps the first persons killed by Holmes in the Castle were Mrs. Julia F. Conner and her eight-year-old daughter, Pearl. Shortly after the Castle was built, I. L. "Ned" Conner went to work for Holmes. He ran the jewelry section of the corner store, and soon the drug store as well. Conner became one of the victims of Holmes' drug store swindle routine—after buying it he found that the fixtures and furnishings had not been paid for. Somehow the persuasive Holmes got back in Conner's good graces, however, and they became better friends than before.

When the police began their search of the Castle, a story appeared in the newspapers that Ned's sister Gertie, a strikingly beautiful eighteen-year-old girl from Muscatine, Iowa, had been killed by Holmes after working for him. Conner vehemently denounced the story as a fabrication, stating that "no one above the level of a slimy lizard or hissing adder could start such a report." "My sister was a pure girl when she died," he added, defensively, "and was not intimately acquainted with that man." Later he admitted that she had worked at the Castle for a few months, but that her death was not related in any way to Holmes and his activities. She quit her job, he learned, when Holmes asked her to marry him, promising to divorce Myrta Belknap and take Gertie to live with him in the East—a proposition she immediately rejected with shocked indignation.

Shortly afterwards, Holmes persuaded the equally attractive Mrs. Conner to work with her husband at the Castle, and taught her how to keep the drug store's books. It was then that friction developed in the Conner marriage. She seemed excessively jealous whenever he waited on a female customer, even as she became increasingly friendly with Holmes, and soon it was *Mr.* Conner who cared for their daughter, Pearl, while she watched the store. Conner told his wife they would have to leave the Castle and start anew if their marriage was to work, and she refused. He left, secured employment downtown, and divorced his wife when it

I. L. "NED" CONNER.
From the *Chicago Daily Tribune*, July 26, 1895, p. 2.

became apparent that their marriage could not be saved and that his wife was having an affair with Holmes.

For a while Conner still kept in touch with his wife and daughter. Holmes would come to him, too, and complain that jealous Julia was not getting along with the customers in the store; Ned would reply that that was Holmes' problem now. Holmes then sent Julia Conner to business college, so she could learn to handle more of the business side of the operation. She began a relationship with one of the men at the college, causing an explosion of jealousy in Holmes, who no doubt was not used to being jilted himself. Then a new mistress appeared on the scene, a fight erupted between her and Julia Conner within two hours, and

JULIA CONNER.
From the *Chicago Daily Tribune*, July 26, 1895, p. 2.

Mrs. Conner and Pearl soon disappeared. Holmes told his janitor, Pat Quinlan, that Julia had married a doctor on the North Side of Chicago and moved to California; he told Joseph Owens, his associate in the phony Campbell-Yates Company, that she had returned to her home in Davenport, Iowa; and he told Ned Conner that his daughter and former wife had moved to St. Louis.

In a lengthy statement to police, Ned Conner said he was certain his wife and daughter had been killed by Holmes—for if Julia were alive, he said, she would be in contact with her family in Iowa. As for motive, it could have been jealousy, it could have been fear that she knew too much and was unreliable, or it could have been insurance. "Holmes was always very anxious to have me get life insurance," Conner recalled, "and my wife was always anxious to have me get life insurance for the child." He never did, however, and suspected that after their divorce Holmes took out policies on both before killing them.

A statement by one of the tenants of the Holmes Castle established that Julia Conner and her daughter were last seen after midnight of Christmas Eve 1891, so that they were probably killed on Christmas day. The family that moved into the room previously occupied by Julia and Pearl Conner found everything as they apparently had left it. Breakfast dishes were on the table, with the victuals, and in the bedroom their clothes were scattered about, just as they had left them upon retiring during their last night there. Pearl's clothes were on a chair. When the family asked Holmes why the previous tenants had left things that way, he replied thay they had been called home suddenly by the serious illness of a sister. The new tenants thought it strange indeed that they would leave that hurriedly and never send after their possessions.

PEARL CONNER.
From the *Chicago Times-Herald*, July 26, 1895, p. 2. Courtesy of the Illinois State Historical Library.

*   *   *

Emeline G. Cigrand was a strikingly beautiful twenty-year-old blond from Lafayette, Indiana, just beginning to earn her living at the new female occupation of stenographer. She was working at the Keeley Institute in Dwight, Illinois, when Ben Pitezel went there to take the gold cure for drunkenness. He brought back stories of her beauty and charm, and Holmes lost no time in offering her a substantial raise if she would come to Chicago to be his secretary and bookkeeper. She was delighted to accept this opportunity for advancement.

101

Miss Cigrand went to work at the Castle in the spring of 1892. She corresponded regularly with her friends in Dwight, and in nearly all of her letters told of Holmes' kindness toward her. He was a "fine gentleman," she said, who often bought flowers for her and once gave her a picture of himself, and even promised to take her to Europe. Then in December 1892 the letters stopped, and no one ever saw Miss Cigrand again. She was, perhaps, the most beautiful of the victims to disappear at the Castle.

On May 1, 1892, Dr. M. B. Lawrence and his wife had moved into a suite of five rooms in the Castle, and when the story of Holmes' true character unfolded in the press they told reporters what they knew—and suspected—about the fate of Miss Cigrand.

"When we moved into the Holmes building," Dr. Lawrence began, "Miss Cigrand was employed in Holmes' office. She was one of the prettiest and most pleasant young women I ever met, and my wife and I learned to think a great deal of her. We saw her every day and she often came in for a few minutes' chat with Mrs. Lawrence. It was not long before I became aware that the relations between Miss Cigrand and Mr. Holmes were not strictly those of employer and employee, but we felt that she was to be more pitied than blamed. He was apparently very kind to her, always buying flowers and presents for her and taking her to the theatre and places of entertainment. He gave her a bicycle and they spent many of their evenings in riding around Englewood and in the parks. They nearly always took their meals together in his office, having them sent up from the restaurant on the first floor. Miss Cigrand did not live in the building, nor did she occupy a flat anywhere with Holmes. He had rooms in private houses at several places, not staying long at any of them."

When did she disappear?

"About the first week in December," replied Dr. Lawrence to the reporter's question. "A week before that time she came to Mrs. Lawrence and handed her a little tin plate on which she had painted a picture of forest scenery. When Mrs. Lawrence asked her why she didn't wait and give it to her for a Christmas present, she replied that she would not be here then, that she was going to spend the holidays with her parents in Lafayette. She seemed delighted with the anticipation of a visit to them. She spoke in the most affectionate terms of them and seemed as happy as a child. When Mrs. Lawrence asked, 'You are not going to stay away from us?' she replied, 'Well, I don't know, maybe.'

" 'Why, Mr. Holmes could never get along without you,' said my wife, laughing.

" 'He could if he had to,' said Miss Cigrand, with a determined expression in her face.

"It had seemed to me for some time," continued Dr. Lawrence, "that Miss Cigrand was changing in her feelings toward Holmes, but I did not think seriously of it at that time. In the light of what has happened since, I believe now that she had found out to a certain extent the real character of Holmes and determined to leave him. The result was that when she told him of her determination he took her life."

"I have not the slightest doubt that Holmes killed Miss Cigrand," interposed Mrs. Lawrence. "If she was alive I know that she would at least write to me, for she had more than the feeling of a friend for me. Nor would she have gone away without saying good-by to me. There was not a day when she did not come to see me, if it was only to open the door and say 'good morning.' "

EMELINE G. CIGRAND.

When did you last see her? Mrs. Lawrence was asked.

"On the fifth or sixth day of December," she replied. "When several days passed, and she did not come in, I asked Mr. Holmes about her.

" 'Oh, she's gone away to get married,' he said, in answer to my question.

" 'Why, that is very strange,' I said. 'I don't see why she didn't mention something to me about getting married.'

" 'Oh, nobody knew anything about it except me and the man she married,' said Holmes. He did not look me in the eye all the time he was talking, and seemed anxious to leave."

Do you think she was killed in the Castle?

"Yes, I do," answered Mrs. Lawrence, "and I'll tell you why. The day after Miss Cigrand disappeared, or the day we last saw her, the door of Holmes' office was kept locked and nobody went into it except Holmes and Patrick Quinlan. About 7 o'clock in the evening Holmes came out of his office and asked two men who were living in the building if they would not help him carry a trunk downstairs.

"The trunk was so heavy the men could hardly handle it. Holmes seemed very nervous and repeatedly told the men to be very careful with the trunk. It was taken down the stairs and placed on the edge of the sidewalk. Presently an express wagon came for it and took it away. Holmes disappeared immediately after and, as we have learned since, went to Wilmette. He did not return to Englewood for two days. The trunk was a very large one; it must have been nearly four feet in length. It was perfectly new, and I am sure it was not the one owned by Miss Cigrand, but I am equally sure it contained her body that night.

"Several days after the return of Holmes," Mrs. Lawrence added, "I again asked him what had become of Miss Cigrand.

" 'This will tell you,' said Holmes, pulling from his pocket a large square envelope which contained two cards—wait, I saved them and will show them to you."

Mrs. Lawrence went into another room and shortly returned with the envelope. One of the cards enclosed read:

MR. ROBERT E. PHELPS.

MISS EMELINE G. CIGRAND.

MARRIED

WEDNESDAY, DECEMBER 7TH

1892

CHICAGO

On the other card was simply printed:

MR. AND MRS. ROBERT E. PHELPS

The stationery was cheap and was printed from type, not engraved.

Did you ever hear Miss Cigrand speak of Mr. Phelps? Mrs. Lawrence was asked.

"No, I did not, and I do not believe that he ever lived," came the reply. "From the very first moment I felt that the wedding cards were fraudulent, and my husband thought the same. He said as soon as he saw it that he believed it was a scheme of Holmes to account for the disappearance of Miss Cigrand without causing suspicion. As you see, there is no address of either party on the cards and no announcement of their future residence. The next day I asked Holmes who Mr. Phelps was, and he replied, 'Oh, he is a fellow Miss Cigrand met somewhere. I do not know anything about him except that he is a traveling man.' Holmes would never say anything afterward about Miss Cigrand unless questioned and then he would only answer in monosyllables. That he killed her I am sure."

There was a touch of morbid irony to the wedding story concocted by Holmes, which Mrs. Lawrence would have had no way of knowing. "Phelps" was the name Benjamin Pitezel used when he underwent treatment at the Keeley Institute and first met Miss Cigrand.

* * *

Minnie R. Williams and her younger sister Nannie played a central role in all the revelations of Holmes' nefarious activities. Born in Mississippi, they were orphaned at an early age. Minnie was raised by a kind uncle in Dallas who treated her as his own daughter and educated her at the Conservatory of Elocution in Boston; Nannie was raised by another uncle, the Reverend Dr. C. W. Black of Jackson, Mississippi, and New Orleans. When the Dallas uncle died, he left Minnie his property, which consisted primarily of real estate in Fort Worth valued at forty to fifty thousand dollars. The two sisters were reunited in Texas until Minnie returned to postgraduate work in Boston.

In Boston Minnie fell in love with a gentleman whose eloquence matched hers. His name was Harry Gordon, and Minnie wrote her younger sister that he was handsome, wealthy, and very intelligent. In March 1893 Minnie moved to Chicago and wrote Nannie that she had married and was now Mrs. Harry Gordon. Harry Gordon was H. H. Holmes.

Minnie invited Nannie to come to Chicago and see the world's fair, an invitation Nannie accepted as soon as her classes were finished in June. On July 4 Nannie wrote to an aunt in Mississippi that she had enjoyed the world's fair a great deal and was now about to embark on an even greater adventure—she, Minnie, and "Brother Harry" were leaving for a tour of Europe. "If I like I will stay and study art," she said. "Write me right away, and address to Chicago, and the letter will be forwarded to me."

As the months passed, relatives of the sisters began to worry when their letters to them brought no replies. Fearing for their safety, they hired detectives to search for Minnie and Nannie. They were especially worried because of the financial transactions that had taken place with the property Minnie had inherited. Holmes, it seems, followed the same pattern in Fort Worth that he had in Chicago. When he arrived in Texas with the deeds, signed over to him by Miss Williams, he filed them immediately for record and began preparations to improve the property. Miss Williams was not with him, but the papers were satisfactory on their face and no suspicion was aroused. Holmes began the erection of a very handsome and very costly three-story stone front building on the land, getting all his material and work on credit. When the building was partly up, Holmes secured $20,000 on mortgages on the property from various banks in Fort Worth. And as creditors began to press him for payment, he left the Lone Star State in a hurry, borrowing somebody's horse in the process of making his getaway.

In November, upon his arrest in Boston, Holmes implicated Minnie in his confession. "When living in Chicago," he told the Boston authorities, "I fell in with a typewriter girl and furnished a house on the outskirts of the city, where we lived together. A younger sister came to visit us and the woman grew so jealous of the sister that in a quarrel one day she struck her over the head with a stool and killed her. To save the woman with whom I was living, I put the body in a trunk, loaded it with stones, and sunk it in the lake [Lake Michigan].

"The woman," Holmes added, "had property in Texas worth about $40,000 and we, Pitezel and I, took it off of her hands and sent her abroad. We never had a legal title to this property, and to save this property Pitezel and I formed the scheme to swindle the Fidelity Mutual Life Insurance Company."

Minnie R. Williams.

As police and private detectives put together the pieces to this puzzle, they found that around June 1, 1893, Holmes and Minnie Williams had rented a furnished flat at 1220 Wrightwood Avenue, on the North Side of Chicago, as Mr. and Mrs. Henry Gordon. Then Nannie joined them, and for several weeks everyone seemed to be happy, taking in the fair. About the end of June Minnie went away, but Nannie stayed with "Brother Harry" and told the landlord that her sister had gone on a trip to Milwaukee.

Minnie stayed away over the Fourth of July holiday. On July 4 Holmes and Nannie went to the fair and took a ride on the Ferris wheel, after which she wrote her aunt in Mississippi. That evening the two were up late and could be heard laughing and joking. On July 5 Holmes went to work at the Castle later than usual, and the landlord saw both sisters walking along the street. That was the last time he saw either one. On July 6 a trunk of Nannie's arrived from Fort Worth, but there was no one present to accept it, and it remained unclaimed later. And on July 7 the landlord received a letter from Holmes stating that business had required a change in location and he would not need the flat any longer.

NANNIE WILLIAMS.

Despite Holmes' confession of Minnie's purported guilt, the authorities were certain that it was Holmes who killed Nannie—and then Minnie as well. While both girls were pleasantly attractive, they were also fairly plump, each of them weighing 140 to 150 pounds—not Holmes' usual type. The real estate, clearly, was the motive. As the police speculated, Holmes urged Minnie to send for her sister, since Nannie might stand in the way of any clear claim to the Fort Worth property. Then, sometime after the noon hour of July 5, he killed both of them.

The question remained, what was Minnie Williams' role in the entire affair? During her months with Holmes her name had appeared in numerous legal transactions. Was she merely a passive, love-stricken heiress who fell victim to Holmes' persuasive enticements, or did this bright and eloquent young lady knowingly decide to join her fortunes with his? Holmes continued to assert that she was alive, afraid to reveal herself after he made public her murder of her sister. But from Minnie there was no word, and the suspicion was widespread that there never would be, at least in this world.

* * *

How many lives were snuffed out in Holmes' Castle? We will never know, of course.

We do know that his turnover in typewriters was rapid—one estimate was that he had employed more than one hundred young women during his years in Englewood; that many, perhaps most of them, were his mistresses for a while; and that on at least one occasion he had his favorite photographed "in the pose and dress affected by actresses," and displayed those to an acquaintance in his apartment.

We do know that Holmes advertised his "hotel" as a suitable lodging for visitors to the world's fair; that no fewer than fifty persons, reported to the police as missing, were traced to the Castle; and that there their trail ended.

We do know that he understood poisons and their use; that the use of corrosive chemicals was a favorite theme in his conversations with the jeweler Davis; and that disintegration of the tissues of a human being through chemical action was another of his favorite topics.

We have the testimony of a witness, his identity protected by police, that he had mounted three skeletons for Holmes from bodies taken from the Castle. One of these, he said, was a man and two were the bodies of women. These were sneaked out of the Castle late at night, and two of the mounted skeletons were returned to Holmes (police had the third in their possession). The witness reported that the flesh on the bodies had not yet been stripped from the bones when they were delivered into his hands, but that the faces were so badly lacerated and torn that identification would have been impossible.

We have the testimony of Mrs. Strowers, a washerwoman who for a while did the laundry for Holmes and Mrs. Conner. Several times, she told police, Holmes came to her and urged her to take out an insurance policy on her life for $10,000.

"Don't be afraid of me," Mrs. Strowers quoted Holmes as saying. "You take out the policy, and I will give you $6,000 cash for it at once."

Mrs. Strowers studied over the offer several days. It seemed fair enough to her, and she was tempted to accept. Friends, however, dissuaded her, and the lucky woman never talked with Holmes on the subject again. But how many others did accept a similar offer, to their permanent regret?

We have the results of the Chicago fire department's chemists when they analyzed the oil taken from Holmes' basement and found spilled on the floor of the huge safe vault in his office. At first appearance it seemed to be ordinary machine oil, with some unknown substance added. But in the course of their tests they applied a small quantity of crude petroleum to the sample of oil and were shocked to discover that the mixture created a vapor capable of causing almost instantaneous death, as it would paralyze the nervous system. Further tests showed that benzine mixed with the oil would result in rapid death; gasoline had the same effect, but was a little slower in action; and even common kerosine, added in a small, closed room, would cause death in a few minutes by suffocation.

Holmes, the police theorized, would place a small quantity of this oil in a bowl, add either petroleum, benzine, gasoline, or kerosine to it, and place it in the vault. Then all he had to do was lure his victim into the trap and shut the door. Death would soon result. A footprint found on the iron door of the vault may have been that of a victim struggling to open the door after spilling the contents of the bowl on the floor.

Finally, we have the testimony of a druggist named Erickson, who told police of Holmes' frequent visits to his drug store and why he thought Holmes was a strange one.

"Well," said Erickson, "he always wanted so much chloroform. During the time I was there, it was only a few months, I sometimes sold him the drug nine or ten times a week and each time it was in large quantities. I asked him what he used it for on several occasions, but he gave me very unsatisfactory answers. At last I refused to let him have any more unless he told me, as I pretended that I was afraid that he was not using it for any proper purpose. He then told me that he was making some experiments and the following day showed me a bottle containing yellow fluid. He had another bottle with a white liquid in it, and when he mixed the two a heavy vapor arose to which he set fire. He also told me that the gas was poisonous. Some time after, when he got more chloroform, I asked him if his experiments were nearly completed and then he said that he was not making any experiments. I could never make him out."

* * *

As we ponder the atrocities bared in Holmes' Castle, which can only be described as the work of a madman, it is difficult to comprehend the ease with which he practiced his sinister activities year after year. We children of the twentieth century are accustomed to seeing our monsters on the screen in appropriately frightening countenance and attire, but Holmes' attire was that of a gentleman and his foremost weapon was overpowering charm. His victims were drugged by the force of that personality long before his chemist's concoctions signaled the end of their use to him. This was more than a momentary tactic, too, as is most apparent in his considerate, loving treatment of his wives even as he was murdering innocent children. For Miss Yoke, there was absolutely no preparation for the shock of his Boston arrest—their home life had been without blemish. Even his Wilmette wife, Miss Belknap, found it impossible to accept the testimony of the castle. She knew that many of his financial transactions were dishonorable, for his victims in that regard included her family and friends, but she could not believe him guilty of the crime of murder.

"In his home life," she would testify to inquirers, "I do not think there ever was a better man than my husband. He never spoke an unkind word to me or our little girl, or my mother. He was never vexed or irritable, but was always happy and seemingly free from care. In times of financial trouble or when we were worried over anything, as soon as he came into the house everything seemed different. His presence was like oil on troubled waters, as mother often said to him. He was so kind, so gentle and thoughtful that we forgot our cares and worries."

And then there was his way with little children. "It is said that babies are better judges of people than grown-up persons," Miss Belknap mused, "and I never saw a baby that would not go to Mr. Holmes and stay with him contentedly. They would go to him when they wouldn't come to me. He was remarkably fond of children. Often when we were traveling and there happened to be a baby in the car he would say, 'Go and see if they won't lend you that baby a little while,' and when I brought it to him he would play with it, forgetting everything else, until its mother called for it or I could see that she wanted it. He has often taken babies that were crying from their mothers, and it would hardly be any time until he had them sound asleep or playing as happily as little ones can. He was a lover of pets and always had a dog or cat and usually a horse, and he would play with them by the hour, teaching them little tricks or romping with them. Is such a man without a heart?"

Even as Holmes was creating headlines in America, England was being shocked by the deeds of "Jack the Ripper." Jack the Ripper, whoever he was, was as real as Holmes and shared some characteristics. But Holmes, it is evident from the testimony of his wives, showed a much greater resemblance to a fictional character of British crime. H. H. Holmes was America's Dr. Jekyll and Mr. Hyde.

7

HOLMES' OWN STORY

Noted Criminal, in Prison,
Writes His Memoirs.

"A SWINDLER, YES, BUT INNOCENT OF MURDER"

Omissions and Contradictions
in His Story Lead
to Skepticism, However.

EXCITING TALE TOLD

How He Procured a Body,
Evaded the Law, and Survived
a Train Wreck in Insurance Scheme.

PRISON DIARY INCLUDED

On May 16, 1860, Herman Webster Mudgett was born in the tiny New Hampshire village of Gilmanton. His father was a farmer of comfortable means, and his mother up to the time of her marriage had been a teacher. Both were devout Methodists, and they raised their three children in that faith. Herman was a thin and scrawny child, a serious and solitary lad who was too aloof to be popular with his classmates. At the same time, he was considered one of the brightest students in the area, and upon his graduation at age sixteen he taught school in Gilmanton and nearby Alton. He eloped at the age of eighteen, marrying Clara A. Lovering before the justice of the peace in Alton.

Years later, while incarcerated in a Philadelphia prison, Holmes would write his memoirs under the title of *Holmes' Own Story*. In reflecting on those early years, he would note nothing out of the ordinary for a country-bred boy. "That I was well trained by loving and religious parents, I know, and any deviations in my after life from the straight and narrow way of rectitude are not attributable to the want of a tender mother's prayers or a father's control, emphasized, when necessary, by the liberal use of the rod wielded by no sparing hand."

He did recall one incident of lasting impression. Soon after he began to attend school, "I had daily to pass the office of one village doctor, the door of which was seldom if ever barred. Partly from its being associated in my mind as the source of all the nauseous mixtures that had been my childish terror (for this was before the day of children's medicines), and partly because of vague rumors I had heard regarding its contents, this place was

117

one of peculiar abhorence [sic] to me, and this becoming known to two of my older schoolmates, they one day bore me struggling and shrieking beyond its awful portals; nor did they desist until I had been brought face to face with one of its grinning skeletons, which, with arms outstretched, seemed ready in its turn to seize me. It was a wicked and dangerous thing to do to a child of tender years and health, but it proved an heroic method of treatment, destined ultimately to cure me of my fears, and to inculcate in me, first, a strong feeling of curiosity, and, later, a desire to learn, which resulted years afterwards in my adopting medicine as a profession."

Reminiscing on some childhood business ventures that failed, Holmes wrote that "the failures were nothing compared with the collapse of the innumerable air castles which had depended upon the result of these speculations." One was a complicated contrivance that, when finished, was to have solved the problem of perpetual motion; another was a windmill so constructed as to make a noise when in operation sufficient to scare the crows from the cornfield. And there was the time he and a friend cleared a farmer's field of weeds for an agreed-upon price. When they finished, he refused to pay, and in retribution they sowed the seeds from the weeds they had pulled all over the field again. "It is, perhaps, a small matter to speak of here, but it so well illustrates the principle that many times in my after life influenced me to make my conscience become blind. . . ."

Curiously enough, Holmes makes no mention of his marriage to his first (and only legitimate) wife, or of their son. After teaching for several years, he planned to enter Dartmouth College. He soon decided upon a medical career, however, and spent one college year at the University of Vermont in Burlington. He wanted to complete his studies at a larger college, so the following September he transferred to the University of Michigan's medical school at Ann Arbor. At the end of his junior year he committed "the first really dishonest act of my life"—he became the northwest Illinois agent for a Chicago textbook publisher and absconded with the funds he collected that summer. Holmes claimed he barely made a profit, but "I could hardly count my Western trip a failure, however, for I had seen Chicago."

At Ann Arbor, young Holmes became intimate friends with a fellow student from Canada. He hints of "many quaint and some ghastly experiences of our medical education"—but fails to tell just what they were, except that "they stopped far short of desecration of country graveyards, as has been repeatedly charged, as it is a well-known fact that in the State of Michigan all the material necessary for dissection work is legitimately supplied by the State."

At last, in June 1884, "I left Ann Arbor with my diploma, a good theoretical knowledge of medicine, but with no practical knowledge of life and of business." The date he gives for his graduation thus agrees with the one appearing in news accounts upon his arrest in Boston. A dispatch from Ann Arbor at that time stated that Holmes was probably a man who had graduated from the medical department of the University of Michigan in the class of 1884. He entered the university on September 21, 1882, giving his residence as Maple Rapids, Michigan. "Some of the professors here recollected him as being a scamp," noted the dispatch. "He had a breach of promise episode with a hairdresser, a widow, who came to Ann Arbor from St. Louis, Michigan."

Life after medical school proved to be a rapid succession of unsuccessful jobs. Holmes nearly went broke teaching school and practicing medicine in Mooers Forks, New York, and learned that his Canadian friend was doing little better. Together they hatched a joint scheme to defraud an insurance company by substituting a corpse. Then, however, he read two accounts of the detection of that type of crime, "and for the first time I realized how well organized and well prepared the leading insurance companies were to detect and punish this kind of fraud." His friend died suddenly, too, and the plan had to be abandoned.

Holmes spent the winter of 1885–1886 as a clerk in a Minneapolis drug store; at this point in his story, he fails to mention his marriage to Miss Myrta Belknap, just as he previously avoided any mention of his first marriage. He moved to Philadelphia, working briefly at the Norristown Asylum and then at a drug store on Columbia Avenue, and in July 1886 moved to Chicago and assumed his position with the drug store of the widowed Mrs. Holton. Here, again, there is deviousness in Holmes' account of

119

his life. He makes no mention of *Mrs.* Holton or her fate, but writes that "I found a small store owned by a physician, who, owing to ill-health, wished to sell badly. A little later I bought it, paying for it for the most part with money secured by mortgaging the stock and fixtures, agreeing to repay this loan at the rate of $100 per month. My trade was good, and for the first time in my life I was established in a business that was satisfactory to me."

Soon his landlord, noting Holmes' success, announced a rise in rent, "and to protect myself I was forced to purchase at a great expense the vacant property opposite the location I then occupied, and to erect a building thereon. Here my real troubles commenced. The expense incurred was wholly beyond the earning capacity of my business, and for the next few years I was obliged to plunge deeply in debt in every direction; and, worse than this, when these debts became due, if unable to meet them to resort to all means of procuring a stay or evading them altogether."

*   *   *

Having been introduced to the era that represented the zenith of Holmes' short but prolific career, we should note once again that *Holmes' Own Story* was written and published during the summer of 1895 as a counterattack against the discoveries in Toronto and Indianapolis and Chicago. "For months I have been vilified by the public press," Holmes cried in the preface, "held up to the world as the most atrocious criminal of the age, directly and indirectly accused of the murder of at least a score of victims, many of whom have been my closest personal friends."

To Holmes "the object of this extended and continuous enumeration of alleged crimes has been apparently to create a public sentiment so prejudiced against me as to make a fair and impartial trial impossible." Thus his own appeal to the court of public opinion, "against the advice of my friends, and in direct opposition to the positive instructions of my counsel, who have attempted in every way to dissuade me from its publication."

For once it is easy to believe Holmes, for it is difficult to imagine his attorneys approving of this strategy. Holmes was not going to be tried in the court of public opinion, but by a jury of twelve men who had been examined and approved by counsel for both sides. In historical retrospect there was little in *Holmes' Own Story* that would withstand the state's impressive evidence that Holmes had murdered Benjamin F. Pitezel. But there was much in it that would reveal the outline of Holmes' forthcoming defense to the district attorney.

As his story unfolds, Holmes elaborates on his experiences in Texas and St. Louis, and on the drama of Minnie Williams' purported murder of her sister. He develops his account of the insurance scheme, Pitezel's "suicide," and his subsequent flight with Mrs. Pitezel and the children substantially along the lines followed later at the trial. The Pitezel children, he asserts, were murdered by Minnie Williams and a friend from her days with the theater, Edward Hatch. Minnie's motive, supposedly, was to strike back at Holmes for rejecting her and marrying another woman, and the mysterious Hatch supinely went along with the plans of the woman he loved and claimed to have married. The ultimate purpose of their ghastly deeds was to place the blame on Holmes and have him hang for their murder.

It was a plot impossible to pull off convincingly, however, for during the summer of 1895 too much had been learned about Holmes. A simple little fact could wreak fatal damage on Holmes' fabrications. In this instance the fabrication was that Minnie became insane with jealousy when she learned that Holmes would marry another woman, presumably Myrta Belknap, instead of her; and the simple little facts were that Holmes first met Minnie in 1893, and he had married Myrta a full six years earlier in 1887—not, as he insinuated, in 1893. This fact of his marriage to Miss Belknap, moreover, was well known among the residents and employees at the Castle, so that Minnie must have been fully aware that he was already a married man, though not a faithful one.

Of the flight through the Midwest, Holmes writes that "Alice did not like to return to St. Louis" and chose instead to remain in Indianapolis while he saw to his business; also that "this form of life [during the flight] was new to the children, and they thoroughly enjoyed it, going about . . . either by themselves, Hatch's or my own company." The children's true feelings were

121

displayed in their touching letters home—letters that Holmes cruelly never mailed—and they speak of boredom, homesickness, and the need for winter clothing so they could escape the confines of their hotel prisons.*

Holmes writes that he took $5,000 of the insurance money to pay for a note that was due on Pitezel's property in Fort Worth and that "the claim so persistently advanced that this note was a forgery is untrue; it was still in existence a short time ago, and if the prosecution will produce it the signature can speak for itself." The prosecution did produce the note at the trial, and the *lack* of any signature spoke loudly of Holmes' treachery against the widow he had robbed.

Holmes writes in detail of his movements in various cities accompanied by the children *and Hatch;* yet at the trial, some thirty-five witnesses from those cities voluntarily came to Philadelphia to testify, and not one of them spoke of another man accompanying Holmes.

Holmes writes that the hole in the basement of the Detroit house was dug by Hatch and that its purpose was to conceal "a package of papers from Chicago." From Detective Geyer's testimony it was established that the hole was about four feet long, three feet wide, and three and a half feet deep—rather substantial for just "a package of papers."

But what *Holmes' Own Story* lacked in facts, it more than made up for with melodrama, and in particular as he describes his homecoming in New Hampshire.

"My pen cannot adequately portray the meeting with my aged parents," Holmes wrote. "Suffice it to say that I came to them as one from the dead, they for years having considered me as such, until I had written them a few days before."

The prodigal son having returned, Holmes toured the family homestead and "for the next two days I tried to feel that I was a boy again, and when I could go away by myself for a few minutes, I would wander from room to room, taking up or passing my hands lovingly over each familiar object, opening each cupboard and drawer with the same freedom I would have used twenty years before.

*See Appendix II: A Holmes Chronology, for the text of some of these letters.

"Here I found some letters written to my mother when I was a boy, and later as a young man; then as a physician, giving her careful directions regarding her health; then the letter written the day before my supposed death, all bearing evidence of the many times she had sorrowfully read them. There also I found toys that years before had seemed so precious to me, and old garments carefully laid away, principally those which I had worn, and which I felt sure mother had purposely caused to be placed separately, thinking me dead, for if such had been the case it would have been the first death in our family.

"And, moreover," he went on, "I had always been looked upon by the others as 'mother's boy.' When I went to the room where, times without number, I had been given such faithful teachings, and prayed with so earnestly, and had I been the earnest Christian my mother had then entreated me to become, I could have prayed for guidance beside the same dear old chair in which she had so often sat with me. I could not stay here, I felt it was too sacred a place to be entered now, and with tears in my eyes, that come again as I write, I reluctantly closed the door and went away."

The reader will be excused for musing that Holmes missed his calling when he chose medicine as his career rather than the writing of dime novels. Restricted by the confinements of his cell from the use of the verbal persuasion at which he was so proficient, Holmes was now engaging in a literary version of what Detective Geyer so aptly termed his "florid ornamentation" and "flamboyant draperies"—of becoming "pathetic at times when pathos will serve him best, uttering his words with a quaver in his voice, often accompanied by a moistened eye, then turning quickly with a determined and forceful method of speech, as if indignation or resolution had sprung out of tender memories that had touched his heart."

Holmes' homecoming tale is sad, indeed, until we pause to remember that it was he and he alone who fabricated the story of his supposed death and who let his parents live for so many years thinking him dead. *Holmes' Own Story*, moreover, still makes no mention of his New Hampshire wife or of his son, now in his teens, who had been raised without a father's love all those years (though in Holmes' case that was probably a blessing for the child).

123

As Holmes languished in prison, his deeds caught the imagination of the American press and his fame spread. On the following pages: the title pages of four books published by and about Holmes catch the flavor of the era and its most villainous character.

HOLMES' OWN STORY

PRICE, 25 CENTS .

which the Alleged Multi-Murderer and Arch Conspirator tells of twenty-two Tragic ... and ... pear- ...

in which he is said to be Implicated, with Moyamen- sing Prison Diary Appendix .

H. W. Mudgett M.D.

H H Holmes

ACCUSED OF MORE CRIMES THAN ANY OTHER MAN LIVING

PHILADELPHIA
BURK & McFETRIDGE Co.
1895

The
Holmes-Pitezel
Case

A

HISTORY

OF THE

Greatest Crime of the Century

AND OF THE

SEARCH FOR THE MISSING
PITEZEL CHILDREN

BY

DETECTIVE FRANK P. GEYER

OF THE BUREAU OF POLICE, DEPARTMENT OF PUBLIC SAFETY,
OF THE CITY OF PHILADELPHIA

———

A TRUE DETECTIVE STORY

———

By permission of the District Attorney and Mayor of the
City of Philadelphia

———

125

··THE··

HOLMES CASTLE

BY

ROBT. L. CORBITT

THE ONLY TRUE AC-
COUNT OF THE GREATEST
CRIMINAL THE POLICE
HAVE EVER HANDLED

ENDORSED BY THE PRESS
GENERALLY

COPYRIGHT, 1895

BY

CORBITT & MORRISON

CORBITT & MORRISON, PUBLISHERS
654 W. 63RD STREET, CHICAGO

HOLMES, THE ARCH FIEND,

OR:

A CARNIVAL OF CRIME.

The Life, Trial, Confession and Execution

— OF —

H. H. HOLMES.

Twenty-seven Lives sacrificed to this Monstrous Ogre's Insatiable Appetite.

PUBLISHED BY

BARCLAY & CO.,

210 and 212 East Fourth St., Cincinnati, O.

THE TORTURE DOCTOR

As Holmes began to be blamed for every crime that had occurred during the previous decade, two *Chicago Daily Tribune* cartoons make the point with reference to an Indian massacre in the Jackson Hole area of Wyoming and Idaho.

HOLMES—"I AM INNOCENT; I HAD NO INSURANCE ON ANY OF THOSE SETTLERS."

"SHAKE, PARD!"

Holmes soon became a man of a dozen faces, if these samples of newspaper art are any example.

Nor is there any mention of how Holmes accounted for his return from the dead. From newspaper dispatches we learn that he told his family that when he left New Hampshire he went west and, while traveling there, had his skull fractured and was robbed of his gold watch and considerable money in a railroad accident. He also lost his memory, he said, and the railroad company—whose name he could never remember—had placed him in a hospital where he was treated for many months at their expense. In this hospital he was given the name of H. H. Holmes, all true identification being lost, and he fell in love with the deaconess who visited him regularly, eventually marrying her. When the name of Herman Mudgett began to dawn upon him, he had an uncontrollable desire to visit his home and his friends, and thus accounted for his sudden appearance back in New Hampshire.

Perhaps Holmes realized this was a story only a mother could believe, and therefore chose not to repeat it to his general public.

* * *

One of the most fascinating episodes in *Holmes' Own Story* involves his tribulations in trying to set up one of his substitute-body insurance frauds. It took place, he said, shortly after the death of his college chum, and the resulting collapse of their plans made him all the more determined to succeed at any cost—but this time working alone. The time apparently was 1887, about when he bought the Englewood drug store from Mrs. Holton and undoubtedly could use all the cash he could get. The chain of events is so unbelievable that the skeptic will wonder if it is all a product of Holmes' romantic imagination, but it remains an exciting tale nevertheless.

While in Minneapolis, Holmes said, he had insured his life for $20,000, payable to his wife. Since "the prospective profits in the work were most alluring," he decided to collect. "Upon figuring up what the gross proceeds had been in similar operations, the result showed me that, with the very modest outlay of $3,950, they aggregated $68,700. This work one can easily see was profitable beyond any legitimate work that might be entered into."*

---

*At the end of this episode, Holmes refers to it as "case No. 5," implying that he had employed this ruse four times before.

The first requirement was a body that resembled him, and so he called on an acquaintance of flexible morals at a Chicago medical college. It was difficult but necessary to find a body that had a "cow-lick" such as his own, "and I had a most gloomy wait, lasting about two weeks, going to the dead room of the college each morning to inspect the 'arrivals' which had come in during the preceding twenty-four hours."

Finally his patience was rewarded. About May 20 he found a suitable body—the man had been killed accidentally falling from a freight car. Holmes made his arrangements with the acquaintance at the college and now had to find a way of moving the corpse. "No chance for detection now could be entertained. No loophole for surprise and discomfiture was to be left uncovered; and I had to do all that was vitally necessary to this end alone."

He went to an expressman whom he trusted completely, only to be surprised to learn that the man had died some time previously. Holmes made inquiries of the janitor of the college and learned that a certain expressman in the neighborhood had done similar "outside work." Holmes called on the man, told him what he wanted, and agreed to pay him five dollars to deliver the body from the college to the Illinois Central station.

They now picked up a specially constructed trunk Holmes had previously ordered for this very purpose. It was an extra large trunk with "the greater portion of it being occupied by a large zinc box of sufficient dimensions to allow a man to occupy it by doubling his joints, where doubling was necessary. This was fitted by a lid of wood to deaden any sound that might be caused through the possible rattling of the ice, which was to surround the inner box. The entire trunk was made water-proof. . . ."

The two of them took the trunk to the college and placed the body in it. The expressman didn't seem to relish that sort of work and once or twice grew pale. And when they arrived at the train station, he announced that, since he had also acted as undertaker and pallbearer, the price had jumped from five to thirty-five dollars—or he would run to the police.

"You may go," Holmes told him, "but first listen to me and answer my questions. Did you not, in the presence of the janitor and myself, help place the corpse in the trunk? Did you not haul it here? Have you not assisted me in all this work?"

133

"Yes, I have."

"That man was murdered. Speak a word about it to anyone, and I will have you arrested as an accessory to his murder."

The driver's eyes widened and bulged, and suddenly he did not need any more money.

Having purchased his ticket for the timberlands of Michigan, Holmes checked his trunk and it began its adventurous trip north. Everything seemed to be going well until the train neared Grand Rapids. Holmes noticed a group of trainmen standing about a trunk in the baggage section, which occupied the forward part of the smoker in which he was traveling. Looking closer, he saw with horror that it was his trunk that had attracted their interest.

Holmes was in a feverish state of excitement when he arrived in Grand Rapids. "As soon as the trunk was deposited in the baggage room, I went in as though to claim it. As I did so, I noticed a stranger looking at me and on the trunk in a manner which made me feel quite uncomfortable. I pretended not to notice him, and thereby got a better chance to study him. I soon concluded that he was a Secret Service man, and that I had been 'spotted.'

"Realizing that some decisive and telling action was necessary at this time, I stepped to the telegraph office and wired myself at the hotel, as follows: 'Holmes. Look after my trunk, which left Chicago this morning. (Signed) HARVEY.'

"The initial 'H' was the same as that on my trunk, and when I got to the hotel, I showed the clerk the telegram, which he held for me, and engaged communicating rooms for Harvey and myself, with a bath attachment. I sent a porter for the trunk, and after seeing it in the rooms, I then learned the cause which attracted the attention of the trainmen to it. My suspicions had been confirmed, for an awful odor emanated from the trunk, and I then knew that the man had been dead longer than the college attendants stated, and, also, that I had been imposed upon."

Holmes locked his room carefully, told the hotel clerk that his baggage should arrive in an hour or so, and stepped out to shop for another trunk. He found a suitably used one, ordered the lock to be changed on it, and while that was being done made several trips to a couple of plumbing shops and bought a considerable quantity of old lead pipe. He had this cut into suitable lengths and made into packages, then placed the heavy packages of pipe in his

134

new trunk and had it sent to his room at the hotel. This was done to make it appear that it was filled with his effects.

The night was warm, so Holmes knew it would not be long before the body's odor would permeate the hotel floor. Hurriedly he bought a waterproof hunting bag and in it carried a large amount of ice to his room, placing the ice in the bathtub. The room had become stuffy, so he raised his window, which opened over the roof of a porch, and noticed that it had grown quite dark.

Holmes was hungry, so he decided to have dinner before proceeding with his work. In the dining room he noticed the mysterious stranger watching him in the reflection of the mirror over the bar.

Back in his room, Holmes prepared a bed of ice in the bathtub and opened the trunk containing the body. "The sight was disgusting, yet when I looked upon it, and realized that at least $20,000 would come to me after a little further trouble, I gazed on it as a very good investment which was about to mature." The monetary possibilities strengthened his resolve, and he placed the body on its bed of ice. Looking at the dead stranger, Holmes found himself "fascinated by the awful solemnity of death," with questions floating across his mind. "Who was he? What had he been? Was he a father, a lover, or brother? Was his absence from home noted? Was he cared for? Or, was he, like myself, a wayward son?"

Holmes' daydreams were interrupted by the sudden entrance of the secret service man, holding a gun on Holmes with one hand and getting out his handcuffs with the other. In the bedroom was a second man, and Holmes noted they had entered through the window. But then the detective ordered his associate to return to the station house, and alone, again, said to Holmes, "This is a nice sort of a business and I have entrapped you neatly in it. It looks very much like the rope for you."

"My dear sir," Holmes replied, "you will let me explain, I hope. This man was my brother. He has just died of a malignant and very contagious disease. He had been sent to a medical college for dissection, and when I learned of it, I determined to save the body from the demonstrator's knife. Come, look again, and see if you cannot discern a family resemblance?"

As the man looked at the decomposing body, his face turned an

135

ashen color, his hands trembled, and the pistol fell to the floor and exploded with a loud report. Holmes grabbed it, turned to the detective, and ordered him to jump out of the window if his life was of any value to him. It was, the man jumped out, and Holmes fired another shot into the air.

This of course brought the landlord and several guests to his door. Holmes closed the bathroom door, opened his door to the hallway, and excitedly told them he had foiled an attempted burglary. They could see a man running in the darkness when they looked out the window. The landlord offered Holmes the use of another room, which of course he declined.

Now Holmes' real work was to begin. He transferred the iron pipe to his first trunk and the next morning placed the body in the trunk he had just bought the day before. He explained to the hotel clerk that he must catch an early train but had left his friend's trunk in his room for his expected arrival. Holmes knew that if the detective were suspicious of his story, he would wait until he left the room and then return, giving Holmes a head start.

Back on a train, Holmes was about thirty miles past Grand Rapids when he got off at a station stop to get a paper. The newsstand was next to the Western Union telegraph office, and as he looked over the operator's shoulder, he noted a message coming over the machine: "Look out for a man and black trunk. Left here this A.M. Arrest and hold him."

The telegraph operator called a boy to take the message to the station policeman, but he was too late. The train was pulling out. Holmes swung on and immediately got hold of the baggage porter. He told him to put his trunk off at the next station, which was just eight miles ahead. This was done, and when Holmes got off himself, he found it a dismal place. It was raining, too, and evidently had been raining all night, for the mud was hub deep on the lumber wagons.

Upon making some inquiries, Holmes learned that he would have to drive to a little town fifteen miles away if he wanted to connect with another railroad. After much difficulty, he found a rig to rent, and carefully attached the trunk to the rear of the buckboard. He did not want a driver, for he knew that this trunk was not waterproof and would have an even stronger odor than the first one.

136

After a grueling drive of seven hours through the mud, Holmes reached his destination and found a combination freight and passenger train about to leave. "It was one of those accommodating trains. I 'saw' [bribed] the conductor, who agreed to hold the train for half an hour. This delay was for the purpose of giving me a chance to freshen my subject up a little. Ice was not procurable, and as there was no drug store in the town, I went down to the grocery store, got the proprietor up and bought several bottles of ammonia, which, when combined with one or two other simple things, made a solution that rendered my quiet friend quite acceptable so far as one's olfactories were concerned."

This operation of attempted preserving was done in the privacy of the baggage car, and all went well until they got about three miles from town. Through the negligence of some section hands, a rail was left without the fishplate being bolted on, and the entire train was derailed.

The engineer was killed, and the conductor was badly injured, as were two or three passengers. Holmes escaped through a window and found the baggage car a wreck. So was most of the baggage. His trunk was intact, though, and he hauled it through the mud to a little shed used by workmen.

When the relief train and wrecking crew arrived, the first man off was the Grand Rapids detective. He had Holmes where he could not escape, for it was now daylight and no trains would be coming or going. "Finally he accosted me, and we entered into 'an agreement' to have my trunk taken to the junction of the road, which was done to my entire satisfaction, and, I have every reason to think, to his also. Just what that little agreement cost me I am not at liberty to say, for that officer still lives."

It was a dark and dreary day when Holmes finally got into the wild expanses of northern Michigan's lumber tracts. He set himself up in a hut, and soon word spread that he was a lumber operator of considerable means. One day he went out in the evergreen forest and failed to return. A week or so later, what was purported to be his dead body was found pinioned to the earth by a fallen tree. Money and papers were found in the clothes on the body that established his identity beyond the question of a doubt.

"Thus," concluded Holmes, "after a great deal of trouble and thrilling escapes from the law's officers, I added the neat little sum

137

of $20,000 to my bank account by September 1st, as I had anticipated."

There was a postscript to this tale, one most appropriate for Holmes. When he had finished with the trunk, he presented it to a friend, but at the time did not tell him of its former use. Some years afterwards Holmes met his friend at his home and told him all about it. Then Holmes' friend and his wife declared that they had often found it open—no one having touched it—when both knew for a fact it had been closed and locked the day before.

*   *   *

A few excerpts from Holmes' Moyamensing Prison diary:

"*Saturday Evening, November 24, 1894.*—A week ago to-day I was placed under arrest in Boston, and after a preliminary hearing was brought here to Philadelphia, where I was confined at City Hall police headquarters. Yesterday P.M. I was placed in a crowded conveyance filled with a filthy lot of humanity, and after what seemed to me an endless drive reached the county prison, located at Tenth and Reed streets, which is known as Moyamensing. I was assigned to a thoroughly clean, whitewashed room, about 9 x 14 feet in size, lighted by one very narrow grated window. The entrance to the room is closed by a small latticed iron door, beyond which is still another solid door of wood, which, when closed, excludes nearly all sound, and thus renders the room practically a place of solitary confinement. A register furnishes furnace heat, and one sixteen candle power electric burner gives light during a part of the evening, it being turned off promptly at 9 P.M. . . .

"I have now had three meals served to me since coming here, and can judge something of what my food will be if I have to stay here any length of time. For breakfast a plentiful supply of plain coffee and a quantity of coarse white bread; at the noon hour a small pail well filled with soup, thickened with barley and a few beans, and containing a large piece of beef; at 5 P.M. I was agreeably surprised at receiving a liberal quantity of cocoa, made, I judge, from cocoa shells—a most healthful drink for one in such close confinement. This was accompanied by another piece of bread, which completed the day's rations. One thing is certain, even if not a great variety, the quantity is sufficient, and is cleanly cooked and served."

"*November 26, 1894.*—My wife came to see me at 9:30 this morning. I had not been allowed to see her since my arrival in Philadelphia, and it required all the courage I could command to go to her under such humiliating circumstances. Our meeting took place in the presence of one of the prison officials. She has suffered, and though she tried heroically to keep me from seeing it, it was of no avail; and in a few minutes to again bid her good-bye and know she was going out into the world with so heavy a load to bear, caused me more suffering than any death struggles can ever do. . . . I am promised that for the present she shall visit me two times a week, each week, not to exceed fifteen minutes in duration. . . ."

"*Tuesday, November 27, 1894.*—My attorney called to see me to-day. He only is allowed to visit my room and converse with me alone. . . .

"I am threatened with arrest upon the charge of murder, if I give bail myself, which is only another form of saying that I must stay here until it is their pleasure to call my case for trial; for if charged with murder, bail would not be accepted. . . .

"Was agreeably surprised to-day to find that unsentenced prisoners are allowed to receive eatables, at their own expense, from outside the prison, and I shall make arrangements to have this brought about. I also can have all newspapers and periodicals I wish. Money here in the prison, aside from these uses, is absolutely without value."

"*November 30, 1894.*—Was instructed to-day that, after I have completed several important business letters I am writing, I must restrict all of my correspondence to one letter a week. All mail is inspected in the prison office. I think my weight is twenty pounds less than at time of my arrest; but I am getting more used to my unnatural surroundings and to my bed of straw, and I am sleeping better. The great humiliation of feeling that I am a prisoner is killing me far more than any other discomforts I have to endure. . . but still feel that I have much to be thankful for, as thus far I have been allowed to wear my own clothing and to keep my watch and other small belongings. The escape from wearing the convict garb I greatly appreciate."

"*January 1, 1895.*—The New Year. I have been busy nearly all day in prison formulating a methodical plan for my daily life while in prison, to which I shall hereafter rigidly adhere, for the terrible solitude of these dark winter days will otherwise soon break me down. I shall rise at 6:30, and after taking my usual sponge bath shall clean my room and arrange it for the day. My meal hours shall be 7:30 A.M., 12, and 5 and 9 P.M. I shall eat no more meat of any kind while I am so closely confined. Until 10 A.M. all the time not otherwise disposed of shall be devoted to exercise and reading the morning papers. From 10 to 12 and 2 to 4, six days in the week, I shall confine myself to my old medical works and other college studies, including stenography, French and German, the balance of my day shall be taken up with reading the periodicals and library books with which ——— keeps me well supplied. I shall retire at 9 P.M. and shall as soon as possible force myself into the habit of sleeping throughout the entire night. . . ."

"*March 1st.*—Commenced to-day to arrange for my trial. Mr. S. P. Rotan is to act with Mr. Shoemaker as associate counsel. Thus far I have devoted but little time to this work, but shall now give my 10 to 12 study hour to it each day."

"*May 16th.*—My birthday. Am 34 years old. I wonder if, as in former years, mother will write me. . . .

"Have retained Mr. R. O. Moon as special counsel."

"*May 21st.*—My case was called in Court today, and I entered a formal plea of 'not guilty.' The trial was postponed until a later date. On Monday, May 27th, my case was called for trial. . . . Theretofore I had not looked upon my case as serious . . . but when the prosecution drew into the case matters altogether foreign to my conspiracy charges, I felt that it could not help but influence the jury. . . .

"I resolved to ask my counsel to allow me to change my plea . . . that while there had existed an agreement to perpetrate a fraud under certain circumstances, there was no active conspiracy at the time when Pitezel's death had occurred, and that the death being genuine, the insurance company had not been defrauded. . . .

140

"Before leaving the Court the Judge stated that I should be allowed the six months I had already been in prison, which I could not but appreciate, as it was wholly discretionary with him. . . ."

"*July 16th.*—My newspaper was delivered to me at about 8:30 A.M., and I had hardly opened it before I saw in large headlines the announcement of the finding of the children in Toronto. For the moment it seemed so impossible, that I was inclined to think it one of the frequent newspaper excitements that had attended the earlier part of the case. . . . I gave up trying to read the article, and saw instead the two little faces as they had looked when I hurriedly left them—felt the innocent child's kiss so timidly given and heard again their earnest words of farewell, and I realized that I had received another burden to carry to my grave with me, equal, if not worse, than the horrors of Nannie Williams' death."

8

H. H. HOLMES ON TRIAL

Alleged Murderer Begins
as His Own Attorney,
But Calls Back Counsel.

DRAMA AND PATHOS

Mrs. Pitezel Tells the Awful
Story of Her Search for Her
Family—Holmes Only Sneers.

SOBS LIKE A CHILD

Prisoner Collapses at His
Wife's Startling Testimony.

THE JURY'S EASY
VERDICT: "GUILTY"

Toronto wanted to try Holmes for the murder of Alice and Nellie Pitezel. Chicago wanted to try him for the murders he had committed there. Indianapolis wanted to bring Holmes to justice for the murder of Howard Pitezel. But Philadelphia had him, and District Attorney George S. Graham said Holmes would be tried where the case was strongest against him. As the evidence uncovered by Barlow and Geyer and others continued to mount, it became evident that that city was Philadelphia.

On September 23, 1895, Holmes was brought from Moyamensing Prison to the Court of Oyer and Terminer in a van loaded with prisoners. But when they reached the courthouse, Holmes did not join the other men, charged with assault and battery or petty larceny or some other lesser crime, in the "cage" of the courtroom. For him a special cell had been reserved.

As it came time for Holmes' arraignment, the courtroom was packed with curious lawyers and spectators. Then came the order, "Put Herman W. Mudgett, alias H. H. Holmes, in the dock." Instantly all necks were craned and Holmes was brought into the room accompanied by two court officers. He was pale and thin, scarcely recognizable as the same jaunty, carefree individual who, a few months earlier, had pleaded guilty to conspiracy. His black double-breasted suit, which was once a perfect fit, now hung loosely from his shoulders, and his collar hung low upon his neck. He wore a vest with a gold watch chain and charm dangling from it. A black pointed beard, grown in prison, hid the sallowness of his face.

Holmes walked to the prisoner's dock with a firm step and sat down. He did not look about the room, but seemed occupied with his own thoughts.

Scene in the court when Holmes was arraigned. From the (Philadelphia) *Public Ledger*, September 24, 1895, p. 2.

"Tell the prisoner to stand up," said the clerk. Holmes arose, leaning on the front rail of the dock, and was joined by lawyers William A. Shoemaker and Samuel P. Rotan. Then the clerk read the bill of indictment in a loud, clear voice, charging Holmes with the murder of Benjamin F. Pitezel. Holmes looked straight at him while he read. At first he appeared nervous; his fingers twitched as he grasped the rail and there was a tremor on his protruding under-lip. But in a minute or two he regained his composure and stood like a statue.

When the clerk was finished, he asked: "How say you, Herman W. Mudgett, alias Holmes, guilty or not guilty?"

"I'm not guilty, sir," replied the prisoner in a low voice.

"How will you be tried?"

Holmes was at a loss for an answer until lawyer Rotan coached him. Then he said, in a voice even lower than before, "By God and my countrymen."

"May God send you a safe deliverance," returned the clerk.

The trial was set for October 28, and Holmes was escorted back to his cell. There he had a visitor, who brought him a message from his aged mother in New Hampshire. "Herman," it said, "tell the truth whatever it may be. Remember the teachings of your mother and the influences which surrounded you in your home when you were a boy."

*　*　*

Monday, October 28, 1895

The trial of H. H. Holmes got off to a sensational start. On this first day, police barriers restricted everyone from the courtroom except lawyers, witnesses, prospective jurors, and newspaper representatives. The general public would be admitted to the gallery, which seated about five hundred, with the taking of testimony on Tuesday.

Judge Michael Arnold, clad in the long black gown that had just recently been adopted by the Philadelphia judiciary, called the court to session at 10:00 A.M. The first display of fireworks concerned the desperate efforts of Holmes' two lawyers, Shoemaker and Rotan, to obtain a delay of two months. Judge Arnold rejected every plea, stating they had had more than enough months to prepare their case. When they saw that their pleas were to no avail, the two lawyers announced that they could not do justice to their client and would withdraw from the case. Judge Arnold refused to allow that, and warned that any

Holmes in the dock. From the *Public Ledger*, September 24, 1895, p. 2.

147

such attempt would be good grounds for disbarment.

Holmes came to their rescue after a short talk with Shoemaker and Rotan. Addressing the judge, he said he wished to discharge his lawyers and obtain new counsel for the following day in court. Judge Arnold stood firm—he would not sanction such a move, he told Holmes, and he warned the lawyers to stay in court unless they were willing to accept the consequences.

Mr. Shoemaker picked up his hat and walked out. Mr. Rotan explained briefly why he could not remain, and joined his colleague. Holmes, thus left alone, requested time to obtain new counsel and prepare his case, but Judge Arnold reminded him that he had advised against the discharge and would brook no delay.

"With that," reported the Philadelphia *Public Ledger*, "Holmes gave up all hope of a continuance and set about handling his own case with a readiness that would have done credit to the most experienced lawyer at the bar. He was cool and collected. Not once did he display the least signs of nervousness. Even when a decision of the court went against him he would accept graciously and make no complaint."

The first order of business was to impanel a jury. Holmes went about his task of questioning the prospective jurors with vigor and appeared most interested in determining whether any of them had seen and been influenced by a "sensational display" concerning him at the Dime Museum in Philadelphia. In a murder trial the defense could challenge peremptorily twenty jurors, in addition to challenges for cause, and Holmes used this right eighteen times. At one point he asked the court if the fact that a prospective juror had formed opinions about the case from reading the newspapers was sufficient cause for dismissal. "It is no longer a reason," Judge Arnold advised him. "It was at one time. It was found impossible in these days to enforce it, as a reason for excluding jurors. Newspapers are so numerous that everybody now reads them, and, of course, they obtain impressions from them. Therefore, unless his opinion is so fixed as to be immovable, the juror is competent. If he says that, notwithstanding he formed an opinion at the time, and had an impression, yet he can try this case according to the evidence, and render a verdict in that way, he is still a competent juror."

At length a complete jury was formed and sworn in, and after

JUDGE ARNOLD. From the *Public Ledger*, October 29, 1895, p. 2.

the lunch recess District Attorney Graham delivered his opening address to the jury. He spoke for an hour and forty minutes, outlining the commonwealth's case in detail, while Holmes sat dispassionately, taking copious notes on his legal pad and referring to his copy of Stephen's *Digest of the Laws of Evidence*. Only twice did he betray an unusual interest in what the district attorney said. When Graham made the forceful announcement that chloroform had been injected into Pitezel's stomach after death, Holmes raised his head quickly and looked at him intently. Again, when Graham told the jury that the prisoner had ruined little Alice Pitezel while she was in Philadelphia—a matter not even hinted at in the preceding days—his face reflected surprise for scarcely a second. He quickly recovered himself and went on with his writing.

The day's session ended with a dramatic confrontation, as Holmes asked to be provided with a list of the commonwealth's witnesses.

"I decline to give that," said the district attorney emphatically. "I will furnish that to nobody."

"Then," continued Holmes, "I repeat my request for an interview with a certain party—the party I spoke of this morning," and observing an inquiring look from Mr. Graham, he exclaimed sharply and with a defiant gaze at the official, "My wife!"

"Which wife?" retorted the district attorney, just as sharply.

"There was a suspicion of tears," noted the *Inter Ocean*, "in the voice of the friendless man, as he responded with a bitterness that was real."

"You well know whom I mean, Mr. Graham. The person you have seen fit to designate as Miss Yoke, thereby casting a slur on both her and myself."

"She will not see you," the district attorney declared. "You had the opportunity to speak to her in my office, but she shunned you."

"I never had," Holmes cried. "I say that I was legally married to this woman two years ago, and there has been no separation except that brought about by you, Mr. Graham."

Judge Arnold advised the prisoner that he would be allowed to write Miss Yoke a letter, which no one but she would see. "You have had every opportunity to speak to her," he told Holmes. "It is indifferent to me whether you see her or not. . . . I will see," concluded the judge, "that you get light and writing materials."

"I thank you, sir, for the privilege," replied Holmes, politely dropping his head.

Court was adjourned, the jurors were locked in their rooms under careful guard, and the man who was accused of being the greatest criminal of modern times was conveyed back to prison to prepare the story that he hoped would save him from the hangman's noose.

*   *   *

Tuesday, October 29

Court opened at ten o'clock, the prisoner as self-possessed as ever. Since he was acting as his own attorney, Holmes' dock had been moved closer to the bar of the court, and a small table, provided with pens, ink, and paper, had been placed there so he might have all the privileges ordinarily accorded to attorneys.

On the district attorney's desk was a large crayon portrait of the man he stood accused of murdering, Benjamin F. Pitezel, placed upright in view of the entire court. Next to this was an equally large portrait of the daughter Alice. But Holmes did not seem to be affected, and his stolid demeanor never left him for an instant.

The first witness was Jeannette Pitezel, also known as Dessie, the oldest of the five children in the family. She identified the portrait as that of her father.

Eugene Smith, the man who had hoped to sell his patent through Pitezel, then testified in great detail about his visits to the Callowhill Street house, the discovery of Pitezel's body, and subsequent developments with the examining physicians at the insurance company headquarters and at Potter's Field. Holmes' scorn was apparent for the man he thought was too illiterate and uneducated to remember his visit to Pitezel's house, but Smith testified that he was positive it was Holmes who came there one day and walked upstairs, with Pitezel following him. Standing in the dock, Holmes leveled his pencil at the witness and did his best to confuse him, but Smith's testimony was unshaken.

The next important witness was Dr. William J. Scott, who had been called by police as they followed Smith back to the Callowhill Street house. Dr. Scott described the scene in the room, the dead man's position and appearance, and what he and the coroner's physician discovered when they later examined the body. He testified that the bottles in the room contained a mixture of benzine, chloroform, and perhaps a small amount of ammonia, of which benzine is explosive. The body had decomposed so rapidly, he said, because the open windows allowed the sun to hit it nearly all day long. And he explained why the doctors were dubious at the police assumption that there had been an explosion. "They argued there must have been an explosion of the fluid in the bottle, but if there had been an explosion there, instead of finding the fragments of the bottle inside, we would have found them scattered all over the room. Instead of that, all these pieces lay inside the bottle. . . ."

As for the corpse itself, "The body laid very peaceful, quiet;

looked as though the man had fallen into a sleep and life had passed away from him without a struggle. His shirt and under-shirt, the pantaloons and under-pants, and stockings, that being the clothing he had on at the time, as well as the shirt bosom was not mussed, and when we were examining his body for money—that is, the coroner's people—you could see that the clothing was not disturbed at all; they were all in nice condition."

Holmes pleads his own case. From the *Public Ledger*, October 29, 1895, p. 2.

Dr. Scott testified further that Pitezel's stomach "was empty, but a fluid found to be chloroform was in his stomach. His lungs showed the odor of chloroform very perceptibly. . . . We came to the conclusion that the chloroform had been used in a large dose, that death was sudden, because we found the heart empty and the lungs congested." In what would be a critical point in the prosecution's case, he stressed again: "His death was very sudden, and the conclusion was chloroform poisoning. Understand, the chloroform found in this man's stomach did not show acute inflammation as it would be if administered during life."

At another point, the significance of which would not be apparent until later, this exchange took place:

GRAHAM: Did you notice the involuntary muscles that were relaxed in this body?

SCOTT: We only noticed that the two sphincters of the bladder and bowels were relaxed.

GRAHAM: Did that occur on the floor of the second story?

SCOTT: Yes.

GRAHAM: That had occurred in the room where the corpse was found?

SCOTT: Yes.

GRAHAM: And the fluid from the mouth you have described, was that anywhere else but in the second story room?

SCOTT: No, sir; and a small stream had run down, filling the grain of the board, from the mouth and the nostril.

The district attorney also asked if Pitezel's death could have been a suicide.

GRAHAM: Could chloroform, if self-administered—could a person taking chloroform have arranged and placed his body as this body was found?

SCOTT: No, sir.

GRAHAM: That could not be?

SCOTT: Impossible.

GRAHAM: Why?

SCOTT: If a man was taking it by the mouth to produce death it would produce more or less spasms with him, it would not be a death from shock immediately, he would not drop and be dead, there would be more or less spasms, he would vomit and fight the dose. If taking by inhalation he could go on for such a length of time, but after that time he would lose consciousness, he would not be able to govern his own will power.

Dr. William K. Mattern, the coroner's physician, was sworn in next and confirmed the points made by Dr. Scott. He added that the body's burns had to be inflicted while the arm was bent and resting on the breast, since the inner part of the arm had not been burned.

GRAHAM: Did the burns cause death?

MATTERN: No, sir; they were superficial.

GRAHAM: That is clear, is it?

MATTERN: Yes, sir; they were superficial. They did not extend into the muscles.

GRAHAM: The cause of death was what you have stated, chloroform poisoning?

MATTERN: Yes, sir; chloroform poisoning.

Holmes in a listening attitude. From the *Public Ledger*, October 29, 1895, p. 1.

Doctors Scott and Mattern, while men of good reputation, were still general practitioners, and the commonwealth now called in its star medical witness, one of the nation's most distinguished analytical chemists. Dr. Henry Leffman, professor of toxology at the Women's Medical College of Pennsylvania, took the stand.

GRAHAM: I want to ask you whether or not it is possible for a man to administer chloroform to himself and them compose himself into such a position as that?

LEFFMAN: I think not.

GRAHAM: Why?

LEFFMAN: No one is aware of the time when consciousness ceases. Judging from my own experience, I have been four times under the influence of anesthetics; there is a condition of confusion before true insensibility comes on, and it would be, I think, impossible for any one to arrange the body in a perfectly composed condition like that entirely by the person's own act. . . .

GRAHAM: Is chloroform easy to swallow?

LEFFMAN: It is rather objectionable—the taste. It is an irritable substance and its taste is of a disagreeable sweet character, so that it is even difficult for persons to swallow it in small amounts. I have occasionally administered it in cases of pain in the stomach, or advised its administration, and I have seen considerable difficulty in swallowing even a small dose.

Dr. Leffman testified further that chloroform taken while alive would irritate the lining of the stomach—a condition absent from the corpse.

> GRAHAM: Would the absense of that irritation indicate that the chloroform had been inserted after death?
> LEFFMAN: . . . It would indicate at least an introduction of the chloroform very near to death.
> GRAHAM: After death would it produce an irritation?
> LEFFMAN: It would produce no irritation after death.

Judge Arnold announced that a night session would be held, and when the court reconvened after dinner, Holmes approached the bench. He had been up until 4:00 A.M. the night before, preparing his case, and had not eaten until 1:00 P.M. this day.

"Partly on account of my physical condition," he said, "partly because I feel I have been annoyed on the trial unnecessarily by reason of not being expeditious in examining witnesses, and partly because of my counsel being criticized, as alleged, for deserting me, I have sent for them in the last half hour, asking them to come here, and if your Honor sees fit to allow them to continue the case, to ask that they will do so."

There was no objection from the bench, and presently the two counselors, looking pale and worried, entered the courtroom. Mr. Rotan began to offer a lengthy explanation when Judge Arnold curtly interrupted and told him, "I do not think any apology is needed."

The first witnesses of the evening session were William Moebius and Frederick Richards, the bartender and the owner of a saloon frequented by Pitezel. Smirks of amusement crossed Holmes' face as Mr. Moebius, a German with a very pronounced dialect, tried to elucidate the difference between "bints and half-bints" and their respective values.

155

Other neighbors testified to their meetings with Pitezel and to the effect that the dead man known as Perry was the one portrayed as Pitezel in the drawing. Dr. Adella Alcorn told how Holmes had rented some rooms from her under the name of Howell, with his wife joining him later and Pitezel paying a visit. John Grammar, a boarder at her house, corroborated her testimony and added that Holmes brought along a girl—whom he identified as Alice Pitezel—when he returned for another stay at the house, this time without his wife. Dr. Alcorn was recalled, and the district attorney began to question her as to whether or not Holmes and Alice had occupied the same sleeping room in her house. Defense objected to this line of examination as irrelevant, and after a whispered consultation between counsel on both sides and the court, the witness was dismissed.

*   *   *

Wednesday, October 30

Seldom, if ever, has a courtroom witnessed personal tragedy of the intensity seen in Philadelphia on this day as Mrs. Carrie Alice Pitezel—her mind numbed, her health shattered, and her heart nearly broken—came face-to-face with the man who had killed her husband, two daughters, and a son in such horrible ways.

Escorted into the courtroom by Detective Geyer, and followed by her oldest daughter, Dessie, and a nurse, the tall, slender woman came dressed in shabby black, with a hat, also black, shielding her pale and worn face. As she spoke from the witness stand, a court crier would repeat her testimony after her, so frail was her physical condition and so weak her voice. Smelling salts were kept beside her, and at frequent intervals she found it necessary to interrupt her testimony to accept a spoonful of medicine that was offered by the nurse.

Often the witness would pause in the middle of a sentence, rest her head upon her hands, and wait several minutes until she could resume her pitiable story. It was an ordeal that would have broken the heart of many a strong man, but she made a hard fight to keep back the tears, and every so often she waited to swallow the lump that kept rising in her throat. It was hard for her to compose herself. But she did so, bravely, until Mr. Graham showed her a letter and asked her whose handwriting it was. It was a letter from Alice, never mailed by Holmes, marked by childish affection for her absent mother and bearing a crude drawing of "Uncle Tom's Cabin," which she had been reading. At the sight of this the mother's heart overflowed.

"Oh, that's Alice's," she exclaimed in a tone that betrayed the agony inside her. As she wept bitterly, there were moist eyes throughout the crowded courtroom and one of the jurors was seen

MRS. PITEZEL.
From the *Public Ledger*, October 31, 1895, p. 1.

157

to fumble for his handkerchief and brush away a tear. It was a scene, it appeared, that touched every heart but one, and that sole exception was the prisoner's. All day he had listened to her story with an expression of the utmost indifference, not once addressing the court, but now a malicious grin formed on his thin lips.

There were other witnesses that day, but none that would come close to matching her impact on judge or jury or curious spectator. Inspectors Perry and Gary of the insurance company told what they knew about the scheme to swindle them and how they unraveled it and located Holmes. Boston's Deputy Superintendent of Police Orinton M. Hanscom, who had risen to prominence as the detective for the defense in the famous Lizzie Borden murder case, told about the arrest of Holmes in his city. Holmes' original confession and the statement by Marion Hedgepeth that broke the case were read to the jury. But it was clearly Mrs. Pitezel's day in court, and her testimony was decidedly damaging to any defense Holmes might offer.

Under the district attorney's guidance, Mrs. Pitezel revealed how Holmes had told her that her husband was really alive and hiding from any detectives the insurance company may have put on his trail. It was Holmes who suggested that she retain Jeptha Howe as her lawyer, and it was Holmes who suggested that Alice make the trip to Philadelphia to identify the substituted body as that of her father, since Mrs. Pitezel and the baby were both sick. He promised that she would be in the good care of Minnie Williams—"his cousin, and the only relative he had living."

After the identification, Holmes returned to settle the disposition of the insurance money. After much fighting, the lawyers—who originally demanded half of the $10,000, threatening otherwise to go to the police—settled for a quarter of the proceeds. Her husband had told her he had half interest in the Fort Worth property, and Holmes warned her that on September 18 a $5,000 note was due on the property. "Mr. Holmes says, 'Come; you've got the money; let's go over in the bank and pay off the note that is due on the Fort Worth property.' . . . We went out to the bank. I don't remember the bank we were in. He went around by the side of the bank. I didn't see him. I had my back to him. He told me to get the money. . . . I got the $5,000, and he came and took it and went around. I looked the money over, and it was all hundred dollar bills, except one was an old note of one thousand dollars. He took the money and went around by the side window, and brought me back a note, saying that the note was paid, and to take care of the note and show it to Ben when I seen him." All she ever realized from the policy was $500, and, being unsophisticated in business matters, she had no way of knowing that the "note" Holmes handed her was worthless.

"You don't want Alice to be alone," Holmes now told her, "so let me take Howard and Nellie, I will take Howard and Nellie to Alice." She should visit her parents, Holmes advised, until he made arrangements for her to be reunited with Ben.

Her next move was to Detroit, after Holmes told her Ben would be there. But when she and her remaining two children arrived, Holmes claimed he had been unable to find a house where they could all meet safe from detectives' eyes. To quiet her concern for the children, he told her they were in Indianapolis, where he had bought a house for his mother-in-law. Since she would not be using it for some time, the Pitezels could stay there rent free once they were reunited. "I said to him when I met him, 'I expected to have heard from the children.' He said I would in a few days; that they would write to me, but Alice was very busy with her school duties."

Then Holmes told her she must go to Toronto to see Ben. She asked if Dessie could join the other children in Indianapolis, never suspecting that the girls were just four blocks away in Detroit and that Howard had already been murdered. "You want to keep Dessie with you," Holmes replied, "because you'll have to go and sign some papers and be with Ben, and Dessie will have to take care of the baby." She had previously suggested leaving Dessie with her parents, but "he said no, that it wasn't good for a young person to be with old people—that I had better keep her with me."

When her husband wasn't there to greet them in Toronto, Holmes explained that he was hiding in Montreal and waiting for word that they had arrived. More excuses were fabricated until she reached a bursting point in Burlington, Vermont. "The second week we were at Burlington, I said I wasn't going to stand it any longer—I wanted to see Ben. I said: 'I believe that you are lying to me, for nothing comes out as you say that it will.' He said he never told a lie to me. I says, 'I don't hear from the children, and you said that I would get the rents from the Fort Worth property, and I haven't got a scratch to show for it.' I says, 'I'm not going to stand it, I'm going to get tickets, and some of these days you'll come, and I'll not be here; I'll go to the children at Indianapolis.' He says, 'No, not until you see Ben.' "

It was then and there, in Burlington, that Holmes left and wrote her a letter from Boston. "[He] told for me to go on to Lowell . . . and for me to go down in the cellar under the potato bin, was a bottle of nitro-glyc—a bottle of dynamite—that it was perfectly safe, and for me to put it up in the attic. . . . Three flights of stairs I would have had to carry it up." She was too suspicious by now and refused—and stayed alive.

The district attorney then asked about her correspondence with her husband and children during this trip.

> GRAHAM: In conducting your correspondence during this trip, how did you mail your letters—who did you give them to?
>
> MRS. PITEZEL: I gave them to Holmes, because he didn't wish for me to send any mail myself.
>
> GRAHAM: How did you get letters that were directed to you?
>
> MRS. PITEZEL: He said that the mail would come through Mr. Blackman [Frank E. Blackman, Holmes' real estate broker], of Chicago.
>
> GRAHAM: Did you execute or sign any orders for him to collect your mail at the different post offices? Look at the paper now shown you.
>
> MRS. PITEZEL: I signed this in Burlington, as I said I didn't get any mail from my parents—I couldn't stand it—and he said that he would send that down to Pat Quinlan, and he would forward the mail.
>
> GRAHAM: These [indicating] are all the same kind of orders, five of them, are they not?
>
> MRS. PITEZEL: Yes, sir.
>
> GRAHAM: You got no mail during that period from anybody outside, did you . . .?

MRS. PITEZEL: No, sir.

GRAHAM: You sent out a number of letters, did you?

MRS. PITEZEL: Yes, sir. He was always wanting me to write, and insisting on it. I said I wouldn't write another scratch unless I could hear from them. . . .

Even the cross-examination by Mr. Rotan, Holmes' lawyer, turned against the defense. It was under his cross-examination that Mrs. Pitezel revealed that her husband claimed a one-third interest in the Castle, and that he had had several arguments with Holmes. "Were not your store bills paid by somebody other than yourself too?" Rotan asked at one point, attempting to demonstrate Holmes' financial generosity toward the Pitezels. "I believe Holmes made some arrangement," Mrs. Pitezel answered, "but my husband said Holmes owed it to him, and if he did not see to his family he would make it hot for him." Another argument concerned the Texas property:

ROTAN: About what time was it that he [Mr. Pitezel] told you he had an interest in the Texas property?

MRS. PITEZEL: I don't remember that, only he said that when he came to Chicago to remove us to St. Louis— told me that Holmes and him had words at St. Louis, and that Holmes wanted to have Minnie Williams come and make out that the Fort Worth property was a fraud. My husband says, says he, "Everything that I have done in regard to that Fort Worth property has been perfectly legitimate, except I have went by the name of Benton T. Lyman," and, he says, "I'll not stand it; if Holmes hadn't taken back what he said, I should have laid him out on the corner." I says, "Benny, please don't do anything. . . ."

A troublesome partner who refused to give up his share of valuable property; who, in addition, frequently hit the bottle and might talk too much about matters best kept hidden; and who, moreover, had been a financial burden for years—a noose was ever tightening around H. H. Holmes' neck.

* * *

161

Thursday, October 31
Friday, November 1

If Wednesday's session was marked by great pathos, Thursday's degenerated to bathos. The occasion was the appearance of Miss Georgiana Yoke—and that was how she gave her name—as a witness for the commonwealth. Holmes' lawyers had protested her appearance on the grounds that a wife could not testify against her husband, but the district attorney produced sufficient evidence to convince the court that Holmes was already married when he purportedly wed Miss Yoke. Since the "marriage" to her was clearly illegal, she was allowed to testify.

Miss Yoke proved to be a tall, slender woman about twenty-five years old, with flaxen hair and blue eyes. She was dressed in black, and was immediately called to the stand as she entered the courtroom. For the first time Holmes broke down. He gazed steadily at her for a few seconds, his hands twitching nervously and his lips opening and closing, but she carefully avoided meeting his eyes. Then he suddenly sank his head into his hands and sobbed like a child. Just as suddenly recovering himself, he dried his eyes and bowed his head, then busily engaged himself with his notes, though occasionally giving way to a sob. It was a performance worthy of his talents.

Miss Yoke testified that on the day of the murder, the man she thought to be her husband had left her about half-past ten or eleven in the morning, not returning until three or four in the afternoon. When he returned he seemed "very much hurried and somewhat worried," and announced that they would leave that night for Indianapolis. He told the landlady they were going to Harrisburg, however, and explained to Miss Yoke that he was concealing their real point of destination because of his financial troubles in St. Louis. Moreover, Miss Yoke recalled, Holmes had a caller the night before all of this happened—a caller he identified as B. F. Pitezel.

There were other fabrications besides the Harrisburg ruse, beginning with the name he gave her when she met him in St. Louis and married him in Denver—Henry M. Howard. At the time of his Texas operations he went under the name of H. M.

Pratt, explaining, she said, that "owing to complicated business arrangements with people with some of his property, he thought it best not to give his own name." He told her they were traveling to Philadelphia to sell leases for his copying process—the "A.B.C. Copier"—and on that fateful Sunday he was supposedly on a business errand. When he returned to Philadelphia the second time, leaving her in Indianapolis while he identified Pitezel's body, he told her it was to close a deal with the Pennsylvania Railroad for the lease of the copier. He used this charade throughout their travels, except that once he said he was meeting a man who wanted to buy the real estate in Fort Worth.

As the district attorney finished his questioning of Miss Yoke, Mr. Rotan announced that his client insisted on cross-examining her personally. The court consented, and Holmes addressed his questions, tremulously, direct to the woman he still insisted was his wife. She never raised her eyes, and gave her replies in whispers that had to be repeated by the court crier. Not much of significance was added, however, by Holmes' cross-examination.

Among the parade of afternoon witnesses were Detective Geyer and Philadelphia's Superintendent of Police Linden, both of whom disclosed what Holmes had told them at various times. Holmes' first real victory during the trial came as the district attorney then proposed to introduce testimony establishing Holmes as the murderer of the three Pitezel children. Rotan objected, and Judge Arnold ruled that "this prisoner is now on trial for the killing of Benjamin F. Pitezel in the city of Philadelphia, and that is the case, and the only case, to be tried here. Evidence of the subsequent killing of these children elsewhere will not be admitted. When the case is over, if it should be found by the jury that the prisoner is not guilty of this offense, he may be sent to Indiana or Canada, and tried for these offenses, but he cannot be tried here. The objection is sustained."

Judge Arnold's ruling had the effect of silencing some thirty-odd witnesses from the Midwest, Canada, and New England who had voluntarily come to Philadelphia to testify for the commonwealth, and who had been supported for six days at the commonwealth's expense. It prevented the offering in evidence of the bones of the boy, Howard Pitezel, the stove in which he was burned, the clothes he wore when he was still alive, the toys he played with, and the trunk which smothered out the lives of the two sisters. It put a quietus, too, on Detective Geyer, who could have kept the jury and audience enthralled for days with the story of his travels.

Thus when court reconvened on Friday, District Attorney Graham wrapped up some loose ends with his witnesses and closed the prosecution's case. He did not even exhibit the skull of Benjamin Pitezel, thereby disappointing a number of spectators in the courtroom whose interest was more morbid than cerebral.

"That is our case" had scarcely fallen from his lips before counsel for the defense rose and made what many persons characterized as "a bold bluff" and many more as playing the last card left. They confidently told the court that the commonwealth had not made out its case, that they lacked the financial means to bring in witnesses for the defense, and that therefore they would submit the case on argument alone.

Court was adjourned until 10:00 A.M. Saturday morning, when the prosecution and defense would present their summations to the jury.

* * *

Saturday, November 2

When the jurors filed into court a moment after ten o'clock, they looked tired and unkempt and there was a thin growth of beard on every cheek. A uniform expression reflected from their twenty-four eyes—an expression telling of resignation to present misfortune, and hope for deliverance in the near future.

At 10:15 Mr. Rotan, junior counsel for the defense, informed Judge Arnold that his colleague, Mr. Shoemaker, was under the care of a physician, suffering from complete nervous prostration. Rotan himself showed the strain under which he had labored. Dark rings encircled his eyes, and his face was pale. He called to the attention of the court a provision of the law whereby the commonwealth had the right to make the closing address to the jury when the defense presented no evidence. Mr. Graham quickly ended the question, however, by waiving his right to the last speech, and thus there would be but one address on each side, instead of two by the prosecution.

As the district attorney prepared to begin his final address to the jury, there was not a vacant seat in the courtroom or in the gallery above, and the doors were locked to prevent the entrance of more spectators. One of the peculiar features of the trial had been the number of society women present to witness the proceedings, and today there were more than ever before. In ordinary murder trials few, if any, women would be present. Celebrities made their appearance, too, and Col. William Mann, the venerable protho-notary whose eloquence as district attorney years before had sent many a felon to the gallows, came into court to listen to Mr. Graham's address, which began at 10:55 A.M. and lasted two and a half hours.

He opened by referring to the relief with which the jury must contemplate the approaching end of the trial. "I am going to ask you," he told them, "to give me your best attention, and your best thought, while I try to refresh your recollection, and aid your reason in reaching right conclusions from the evidence." If they were not satisfied when he was finished that the prisoner had committed this crime, they should acquit him and set him free. "The Commonwealth is bound to prove its case from the initial step, down to the very last syllable of testimony requisite to make it complete. The Commonwealth has done so in this case. The Commonwealth has proved by testimony every step in this im-portant proceeding, out of the lips of thirty-five witnesses who have been examined before you. We have endeavored to establish it link by link, one by one, each one separate and distinct from the others but together making the chain complete and perfect."

The district attorney then reviewed the evidence in detail, beginning with the testimony related to the events at the Callowhill Street house. "Of course, the Commonwealth wanted to show that the prisoner had been there; that he knew this house; that he was in the habit of visiting it; that he was not a stranger to Pitezel"—and that had been demonstrated beyond a doubt.

Mr. Graham next reviewed the medical testimony indicating the "absense of struggle and a condition of perfect tranquility and repose." He took up Holmes' allegation in his confession that he had found the body on the third floor and moved it to the second, rigging a suicide to look like an accident. "There was a fecal discharge, and the bladder also was empty. These were the results of a condition that comes on when death is imminent. . . . That, gentlemen of the jury, was the condition of this body *on the second floor* of this house—the flow from the mouth, and the other discharges from his person *occurred on that floor.* The dead man died there. There was no trace of any discharge on the third-story floor." As for the purported explosion, "Even the smartest, even the brightest, even the keenest criminal will make mistakes, and when Holmes broke that jar, he broke it leaving the glass particles or fragments lying *inside* the bottle, whereas an explosion would have scattered them all about the room. . . .

"I want you to remember," he told the jurors, "at this stage of the argument, that the Commonwealth has established one fact beyond contradiction, which is that this dead man was killed by the use of chloroform poisoning. Two witnesses have sworn to this fact—no one has contradicted them—and the defense admits that this was the cause of death." In addition to this there was the testimony of Dr. Leffman, "one of the most distinguished analytical chemists perhaps in this country," proving "not only that this man was poisoned with chloroform poison, but that the chloroform poison was not self-administered. In other words, that the deceased did not commit suicide. . . .

"Now the Commonwealth must proceed to show you," he continued, "for we can assume nothing, that the dead man was Benjamin F. Pitezel." That completed, Graham reviewed how Holmes had reacted when returning from the Callowhill Street house to his wife. "Why did he go away hastily? Why did he conceal the place of his destination? Was it because all that transpired on that Sunday in No. 1316 Callowhill Street was haunting him and pursuing him?"

Step by step, the district attorney outlined the motives—the insurance conspiracy, the arguments between Holmes and Pitezel, the danger Pitezel represented to the prisoner. When he came to the story of Mrs. Pitezel, he vowed that "in all the fifteen years of my service in this office, I do not remember a story that stirred my heart or moved my sensibilities like the broken sentences of that woman, when, with evident suffering in every line and mark upon her face, in the supreme effort that she made to control herself, and to avoid breaking down, she told that pitiful, yet marvelous story, of how this man led her from place to place in the pursuit of her husband. I do not see, for the life of me, how he could sit there in the dock unmoved and look her in the face, conscious, as he must be, of the awful wrong that he has perpetrated upon her—how he could sit there and look her in the face, and listen to the harrowing tale of suffering and agony, without wincing, without changing a muscle—he is a man of steel, with a heart of stone, and remains utterly unmoved.

"Gentlemen," the district attorney continued, "there was once during the course of this trial that tears seemed to come to his eyes, and he appeared to be moved when Miss Yoke came upon the witness stand the first day. But it was a subject of such universal comment that you must have noticed it as well as I and others, that when she was recalled to the stand the second day, no tear dimmed his eye. The questions of his lawyers showed that the tears of the first day were summoned to influence her; to excite her pity for him so that in telling her story she might be induced to favor him. But on the second day, when his lawyer's shafts were dipped in malice, and question upon question was thrust at her regardless of how they placed her before the world or the community, he sat as stony, as immovable, as when Mrs. Pitezel told her pitiful story from the witness box.

"That was a strange story, gentlemen; if you and I had read it in fiction, we would say, perhaps, that the novelist had overdrawn or overstated the facts; that he had overdrawn the story, and made it stronger than our imagination or fancy could tolerate."

Nearing his conclusion, the district attorney reviewed what had been accomplished. "We have established that this is Benjamin F. Pitezel; we have established that he has died of chloroform poisoning; we have established that that was not self-administered, but administered by a second person; we have shown that he was there in that house on that fateful Sunday alone with the dead man; we have shown that every story told by him to explain his presence was false; we have shown that his theory and therefore his allegation of suicide was false; we have shown the effort at concealment when there was no other object unless it be that the defendant knew he had committed a murder and was telling these falsehoods, one after the other, to conceal it. Upon no other hypothesis can his conduct be explained than that he was concealing the crime of murder. That is what made him flee from city to city; that is what made him take his wife with him upon this wonderful journey; that is what made him take even the children along; that is what made him conceal the letters and that is what made him shut off communication between the different members of that household. This man was fleeing from the shadow of murder; that was the crime he was seeking to avoid; that was what he was fleeing from. It was the menace of pursuit and detection that made him take this journey which, if it had not been interrupted at Boston, would only have terminated when he reached Berlin with his alleged wife, Miss Yoke.

"Now this strange trial is drawing rapidly to a close," he added, and several degrees of guilt might be found. But—and Holmes appeared to shrink from the accusing finger and thunderous tones of the district attorney—but "there is no middle ground in this case. It is the highest crime known to the law under the circumstances surrounding the deceased, for he was poisoned to death, and the poisoning itself indicates a clear intent to kill."

"I know," the district attorney told the jurors in conclusion, "that great stress will be laid upon 'A reasonable doubt.' [and] 'If you have a doubt this man is entitled to the benefit of it.' So he is, but it must not be a doubt suggested by the desire to avoid the performance of an unpleasant duty. If the evidence fails to make the case out he is entitled to his acquittal, but you are asked to perform no higher function here than in your own home or office or place of business. If this evidence would convince you as men outside of this court of this man's guilt it ought to convince you equally in the jury box."

* * *

The afternoon session began after a luncheon recess, and Mr. Rotan, after a moment's conversation with Holmes, began the argument for the defense. He was self-possessed and received admiration for the pluck and endurance with which he fought practically single-handedly against the mighty force of the commonwealth's evidence and the skill and experience of the district attorney. With his senior colleague under a doctor's care, he was entirely alone.

The young lawyer made the best of a hopeless situation, being forced to concede, as he did, that the dead man was indeed Pitezel, that Holmes had hatched a scheme of fraud with the deceased, that his client was present at the Callowhill Street house on the day of the death, and that there had been no explosion. The narrow question to be decided, he told the jury, was whether Pitezel's death *could* have been a suicide—and he tried valiantly to defend the scenario painted by Holmes—and if not, whether there was conclusive proof that it was Holmes who killed him. Mr. Rotan concluded by reminding the jury that Holmes chose to be brought to Philadelphia on the charge of conspiracy rather than be taken to Fort Worth, where he was wanted for stealing a horse. Would any man have made such a choice, he demanded, if he risked being accused also of murder? Would he avoid a trivial charge in a far distant place—and "they never lynch a man for stealing a horse, even in Texas"—to put his neck in danger by coming voluntarily to Philadelphia?

"I now let this case go to you with a great deal of confidence," he concluded, "so much confidence that we have not put in a defense. We feel that the Commonwealth has failed in removing that reasonable doubt to which the prisoner is entitled, and that we can safely rely upon this case going to you and your rendering a verdict of not guilty. This poor man has indeed suffered long, and undoubtedly will suffer, if not here, in other places, for a long time to come, and I only ask of you that you decide this case upon the facts here presented, which, if you do, we have no fear but that you will render a verdict of acquital [sic]."

Mr. Rotan concluded his address at 4:30 P.M. and Judge Arnold charged the jury. He began with the usual definition of the various degrees of murder and manslaughter and read several passages from the penal code of Pennsylvania. He instructed the jury to direct their thoughts to the question whether the prisoner had committed murder, and, if so, of what degree. If the commonwealth had proved that it was a willful, deliberate, and premeditated murder, then he was guilty of murder in the first degree—a crime punishable by death.

"The testimony offered," said the judge, "is known in law as circumstantial evidence, as distinguished from direct testimony, or the evidence of eye witnesses to the offense. Of this kind of testimony I will say that many of the most important cases are proved by circumstantial evidence only. . . .

"The word 'circumstantial,' " Judge Arnold noted, "leads some persons to believe that the evidence is inconclusive and imperfect, but this is not so. The difference between circumstantial and direct evidence is that direct evidence is more immediate, the evidence of the eyesight, generally, and requires fewer witnesses than a chain of circumstances which leads to but one conclusion. And so far as falsehood and perjury are concerned, it is quite as likely, and sometimes easier, to commit perjury and convict by direct evidence than it is to convict by perjury in circumstantial evidence; for proof of the latter kind is an inference or a presumption from a series of facts which must be fitted together as to make a continuous story, and this requires a greater number of witnesses generally, thereby rendering it more difficult to falsify and easier to detect the falsehood, if it is attempted. . . .

"In cases of killing by means of poison," the judge further explained, "experience shows that nearly all such cases are proved by circumstantial evidence only. Poisoning is generally a secret act. . . ."

Thus at 5:40 in the afternoon Holmes' fate passed into the hands of the jury. The twelve men were immediately taken to their deliberating room, under the escort of a corps of court officers, and the best efforts of the "tipstaves" could not quell the buzz of excitement that arose in the courtroom. Holmes was taken back to his cell, and although a smile was on his lips, it was clear that he was extremely nervous. Judge Arnold said he would remain in the building until midnight, if necessary, and if no verdict had been reached by that time he would come to court at ten o'clock the next morning.

Nobody believed it would come to that, however. Interest was at fever heat, and many wagers were made as to the nature of the verdict. In spite of the late hour, not an empty seat was to be found within the four walls, nor was one relinquished even during the recess that followed.

At twenty minutes of nine there was a bustle of moving people as it became known that the jury was returning. A moment later Judge Arnold took his seat. District Attorney Graham and his assistants entered and the jury filed solemnly in and took their seats in the box. Then, amid an oppressive silence, Holmes was brought in and placed in the dock. For a moment there was not a sound. The man who was about to hear his doom pronounced stood erect in the dock, the same deathlike pallor, which could grow no deeper, on his face. He stared at the jury blankly, his hands clasped behind his back. Once or twice he moistened his lips with his tongue. There was no other sign of agitation.

Then, from the deep-voiced court clerk, came the words: "Jurors, look upon the prisoner; prisoner, look upon the jurors. How say you, gentlemen of the jury, do you find the prisoner at the bar, Herman W. Mudgett, alias H. H. Holmes, guilty of the murder of Benjamin F. Pitezel or not guilty?"

The condemning syllables came promptly from the foreman: "Guilty of murder in the first degree."

"Ahem," uttered Holmes, clearing his throat, but his shrunken form never trembled, his lips betrayed no quiver, and his marvelous nerve did not forsake him. There was only a tighter clasp of the hands folded behind him. Then he slowly sat down, and at the request of counsel, the jury was polled—that is, each of the twelve men separately listened to the clerk's query and responded with his finding. As each name was called, Holmes wrote it on the margin of a newspaper in his hand, and the fingers holding the pencil never shook. One of these jurors would later reveal that they had reached their verdict before the doors of their room closed behind them. But, however atrocious the crime and however fiendish the criminal, it is hard to send a man to the gallows in one minute's time, and so for decency's sake they waited until after dinner to announce their readiness.

The verdict was formally recorded by the court; the usual motions for a new trial were made by counsel for the defense —they would not, in the end, succeed; and the jury was thanked for their attention and labors and sent home. With that the court adjourned, and the trial described as "the most extraordinary case in the annals of American courts" was over.

9
HOLMES CONFESSES

The Most Awful Story of
Modern Times Told by the
Fiend in Human Shape.

HIS VICTIMS NUMBER
TWENTY-SEVEN

Every Detail of His Fearful Crimes
Told by the Man Who Admits
He is Turning into the Shape
of the Devil.

A GREAT BURDEN REMOVED;
CONVERTS TO CATHOLIC FAITH

On April 9, 1896, less than a month before he would die by the rope, Herman Webster Mudgett, under his alias of H. H. Holmes, signed his name to a lengthy statement in which he told in gruesome detail how he murdered twenty-seven people and attempted to take the lives of six others. It was a confession bold and dramatic and tragic enough to be accepted as a fitting culmination to the sudden twists and turns of his previous lines of defense, to the appalling discoveries in Toronto and Indianapolis and Chicago, and to the great confrontation in the Philadelphia courtroom. His execution would almost appear anticlimactic, for any expiation in this realm would have to seem insufficient to atone for such pervasive evil.

There were those who said it was all too neat; that Holmes, knowing he could no longer hide his responsibility for the deaths of four members of the Pitezel family, was now determined to go all out in the opposite direction and guarantee himself a place in history as the most horrendous of all criminals. With its grandiloquence it seemed appropriate that William Randolph Hearst would syndicate the confession to the press, and the skeptics saw a pecuniary advantage for Holmes—to the tune of $10,000, it was said—to make it as dramatic as he could. It was also true that certain details of Holmes' confession seemed to be contradicted by facts uncovered elsewhere. Still, there was that earthen grave in a Toronto cellar and the stove outside Indianapolis stained with human grease, as well as the laboratory of crime on Sixty-third Street—for such a monster, was this confession really all that implausible?

There was its apparent effect on Holmes, too. To those who saw him in his prison cell, it was evident that his confession had removed a great burden. He turned introspective, even serene, and announced his conversion to the Catholic faith. In each cell was a stout iron chain, such as is used to manacle unruly prisoners, fastened to a staple in the floor. Holmes took the chain in his cell and arranged it in the form of the cross. Father Dailey, of the Church of the Annunciation, became Holmes' constant attendant.

But if the confession were genuine, why would he then retract it at the last moment, as he stood on the gallows, and for one final time declare his innocence? Were we again witnessing a desperate battle within one soul, Holmes' Mr. Hyde boasting of great evil and his Dr. Jekyll protesting innocence?

* * *

As he opened his confession, Holmes praised the work of Assistant District Attorney Barlow, Detective Frank Geyer, and Inspector O. Le Forrest Perry, remarking that "it seems almost impossible that men gifted with only human intelligence could have been so skillful." He conceded that the recital he was about to make would brand him as "the most detestable criminal of modern times," but insisted that among the reasons for his decision to go ahead "are not those of bravado or a desire to parade my wrongdoings."

His first murder, said Holmes, was that of Dr. Robert Leacock of New Baltimore, Michigan. Leacock was a friend and former schoolmate, and Holmes killed him for his $40,000 in life insurance. "Prior to this death, which occurred in 1886, I beg to be believed in stating that I had never sinned so heavily either by thought or deed. Later, like the man-eating tiger of the tropical jungle, whose appetite for blood has once been aroused, I roamed about the world seeking whom I could destroy."

The next victim was a tenant of the Castle, Dr. Russell. During a controversy concerning the payment of Russell's rent, Holmes struck him to the floor with a heavy chair and Russell, with one cry for help ending in a groan of anguish, ceased to breathe. It was with this victim that Holmes began his practice of selling the bodies to an acquaintance at a Chicago medical college, receiving from twenty-five to forty-five dollars for each acceptable corpse.

Victims three and four were Mrs. Julia Conner and her daughter Pearl. Mrs. Conner's death, he said, was to a certain extent due to a criminal operation, with another man and a woman—who remained anonymous—sharing the responsibility with Holmes for both the operation and the death. Pearl he poisoned, in fear that she was old enough to understand too much about her mother's death.

A man named Rodgers, of West Morgantown, Virginia, became Holmes' fifth victim during a fishing trip. Learning that his companion had some money, Holmes ended his life by a sudden blow upon the head with an oar.

The next case was that of Charles Cole, a Southern speculator. Holmes had the assistance of a confederate on this one, who struck him so hard on the head that his skull was crushed and thus useless to the medical college. Tantalizing the police and his readers, Holmes refused to name his confederate but allowed that "this is the first instance in which I knew [he] had committed murder, though in several other instances he was fully as guilty as myself, and, if possible, more heartless and blood-thirsty. I have no doubt he is still engaged in the same nefarious work, and if so is probably aided by a Chicago business man."

A domestic named Lizzie became the seventh victim. Over the years, Holmes had promoted Pat Quinlan from janitor to han-dyman to confidant, and now Quinlan was paying her too close attention. Afraid that Quinlan, a married man, might leave his job and run off with Lizzie, Holmes thought it wise to end the life of the girl. She was the first one he suffocated in the vault.

The eighth, ninth, and tenth cases were Mrs. Sarah Cook, her unborn child, and her niece Miss Mary Haracamp, who became a stenographer for Holmes. Mrs. Cook and Miss Haracamp had access to all the rooms by means of a master key and one evening burst into a room as Holmes was busily engaged preparing his last victim for shipment. "It was a time for quick action, rather than for words of explanation upon my part, and before they had recovered from the horror of the sight, they were within the fatal vault. . . ."

177

Miss Emeline Cigrand then filled the vacancy for a stenographer. Holmes found it "particularly obnoxious" when she told him of her engagement to a fellow, "both because Miss Cigrand had become almost indispensable in my office work, and because she had become my mistress as well as stenographer." He killed her on the day she was getting married, when she came to his office to bid him good-bye. "While there I asked her to step inside the vault for some papers for me." Holmes promised to release her if she wrote a letter to her financee ending their relationship. "She was very willing to do this and prepared to leave the vault upon completing the letter only to learn that the door would never be again opened until she had ceased to suffer the tortures of a slow and lingering death."

Then followed an unsuccessful attempt to collect ninety dollars for three "stiffs" by murdering three young women who worked in his restaurant. His mistake was in attempting to chloroform all three at the same time, and they overpowered him and escaped.

The twelfth victim was the very beautiful Rosine Van Jassand, whom he induced to come into his fruit and confectionery store. Once he had her within his power, Holmes compelled her to live with him. In time he killed her by administering ferrocyanide of potassium and burying her in the basement.

Robert Latimer, who had been Holmes' janitor for some years, was next. Knowing of Holmes' insurance schemes, he tried extortion and lost. "I confined him within the secret room and slowly starved him to death. . . . Finally, needing its use for another purpose and because his pleadings had become almost unbearable, I ended his life. The partial excavation in the walls of this room found by the police was caused by Latimer's endeavoring to escape by tearing away the solid brick and mortar with his unaided fingers."

The fourteenth death was that of Miss Anna Betts, and was caused by his purposely substituting a poisonous drug in a prescription that she filled at his drug store. He killed Miss Gertrude Conner, of Muscatine, Iowa, in the same way, though his role was not suspected at the time because the poison did not kill her until a month after she had returned home.

The sixteenth murder was a young woman from Omaha with valuable real estate holdings in Chicago. Convincing her that a favorable opportunity had come for her to convert her holdings into cash, and doing so for her, he persuaded her to come to Chicago and he paid her the money, taking a receipt and thus protecting himself in case of an inquiry at a later date. She died in the vault, and he of course got back the money.

Following this was the death of Mr. Warner of the Warner Glass Bending Company. "It will be remembered," Holmes wrote, "that the remains of a large kiln made of fire brick was found in the Castle basement. It had been built under Mr. Warner's supervision for the purpose of exhibiting his patents. It was so arranged that in less than a minute after turning on a jet of crude oil atomized with steam the entire kiln would be filled with a colorless flame, so intensely hot iron would be melted therein. It was into this kiln that I induced Mr. Warner to go with me, under pretense of wishing certain minute explanations of the process, and then stepping outside, as he believed to get some tools. I closed the door and turned on both the oil and steam to their full extent. In a short time not even the bones of my victim remained."

About this time Holmes became associated with a young Englishman who had a great knack for manipulating real estate securities to obtain a good commercial rating. When a wealthy banker named Rodgers arrived from a north Wisconsin town, they brought him to the Castle's secret room and, by alternately starving him and nauseating him with the gas, forced him to sign checks and drafts they had prepared totaling $70,000. The partner administered chloroform, and Holmes disposed of the body with the medical college.

Holmes could not even remember the name of his nineteenth victim—a wealthy woman who lived above the restaurant. Chloroform was his weapon there, too.

The Williams sisters came next. His murder of Minnie, Holmes said, was "without exception the saddest and most heinous of any of my crimes," and he begged his readers not to believe any of the vile stories he had spread about her character. "What has been said by her Southern relatives regarding her pure and Christian life should be believed; also, that prior to her meeting me in 1893 she was a virtuous woman."

He first met Minnie in New York in 1888, Holmes explained, where she knew him as—Edward Hatch. "Soon after entering my employ I induced her to give me $2,500 in money and to transfer to me by deed $50,000 worth of Southern real estate and a little later to live with me as my wife, all this being easily accomplished owing to her innocent and child-like nature. . . . I also learned that she had a sister Nannie in Texas who was an heir to some property and induced Miss Minnie Williams to have her come to Chicago upon a visit."

Holmes killed Nannie at the castle, after forcing her to assign to him all she possessed. "It was the foot-print of Nannie Williams . . . that was found upon the painted surface of the vault door made during her violent struggles before her death." Holmes then took Minnie on a trip to Momence, Illinois. About eight miles east of the town he poisoned her and buried her body in the basement of a house.

The twenty-second victim was a man who came to visit the world's fair, and whose name Holmes could not recall. "I determined to use this man in my various business dealings, and did so for a time, until I found he had not the ability I had at first thought he possessed, and I therefore decided to kill him." He buried the body in a basement of another house he owned in Chicago.

"After Miss Williams' death I found among her papers an insurance policy made in her favor by her brother, Baldwin Williams, of Leadville, Colorado. I therefore went to that city early in 1894, and, having found him, took his life by shooting him, it being believed I had done so in self-defense." Baldwin Williams would be Holmes' last victim outside of the Pitezel family.

* * *

Of Benjamin F. Pitezel, victim number twenty-four, Holmes wrote that from the first hour of their acquaintance, "I intended to kill him, and all my subsequent care of him and his, as well as my apparent trust in him by placing in his name large amounts of property, were steps taken to gain his confidence and that of his family so when the time was ripe they would the more readily fall into my hands. . . .

"It seems almost incredible now as I look back," Holmes reflected, "that I could have expected to have experienced sufficient satisfaction in witnessing their deaths to repay me for even the physical exertion that I had put forth in their behalf during those seven long years, to say nothing of the amount of money I had expended for their welfare, over and above what I could have expected to receive from his comparatively small life insurance. Yet, so it is. . . ."

Knowing of Pitezel's return to the bottle, Holmes forged discouraging letters from Mrs. Pitezel and mailed them to his associate at the Callowhill Street address. Pitezel became despondent, as Holmes knew he would, and when Holmes was ready to make his move, his accomplice was conveniently and insensibly drunk.

"Only one difficulty presented itself," Holmes wrote. "It was necessary for me to kill him in such a manner that no struggle or movement of his body should occur, otherwise his clothing being in any way displaced it would have been impossible to again put them in a normal condition. I overcame this difficulty by first binding him hand and foot and having done this I proceeded to burn him alive by saturating his clothing and his face with benzine and igniting it with a match. So horrible was this torture that in writing of it I have been tempted to attribute his death to some more humane means—not with a wish to spare myself, but because I fear that it will not be believed that one could be so heartless and depraved. . . .

"The least I can do," Holmes went on, "is to spare my reader a recital of the victim's cries for mercy, his prayers and finally, his plea for a more speedy termination of his sufferings, all of which upon me had no effect. Finally, when he was dead I removed the straps and ropes that had bound him and extinguished the flames and a little later poured into his stomach one and one-half ounces of chloroform. . . . I placed it there so that at the time of the post mortem examination, which I knew would be held, the coroner's physician would be warranted in reporting that the death was accidental. . . ."

One result he had not expected, however. The chloroform "drove from his entire body tissue, brains and viscera, all evidence of recent intoxication to such an extent that the physicians who examined the body . . . did not believe the man was drunk at the time of his death, or within twelve hours thereof."

Why did he make no defense at his trial? Holmes answered that as a result of Detective Geyer's discoveries, "which we could not at that time in any way refute," and of Dr. Leffman's learned testimony that no one could or had ever been known to lose consciousness by chloroform self-administered, "it would have been but a waste of my counsel's energies, and of my own, to have tried to convince the most impartial juries that it was a case of suicide and not a murder."

Holmes asked himself a second question as well—did Pitezel know of his previous acts of murder, and had he participated in them? "I answer that he neither knew of nor was a party to the taking of any human life. . . . The worst acts he ever participated in were dishonesties regarding properties and unlawful acts of trade, in which he aided me freely." And not being aware of Minnie Williams' death, Pitezel sincerely planned to have Alice attend a school he believed she was opening near Boston.

Of the Irvington tragedy, which came next, Holmes wrote that around 6:00 P.M. on the day of October 10 he called Howard Pitezel into the house "and insisted that he go to bed at once, first giving him the fatal dose of medicine. As soon as he had ceased to breathe I cut his body into pieces that would pass through the door of the stove and by the combined use of gas and corncobs proceeded to burn it with as little feeling as 'tho it had been some inanimate object."

And in Toronto, on the afternoon of October 25, he took Alice and Nellie Pitezel "to the Vincent Street house and compelled them to both get within the large trunk, through the cover of which I made a small opening. Here I left them until I could return and at my leisure kill them. At 5:00 P.M. I borrowed a spade of a neighbor and at the same time called on Mrs. Pitezel at her hotel. I then returned to my hotel and ate my dinner, and at 7:00 P.M. went

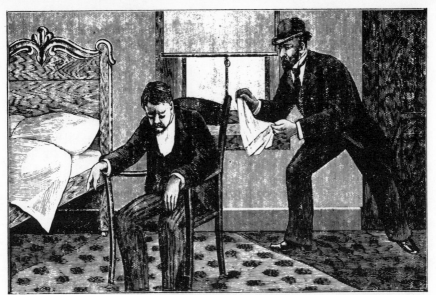

Holmes sneaked up to the sleeping man. The next instant the handkerchief was bound tightly about the head of the doomed man.

again to Mrs. Pitezel's hotel, and aided her in leaving Toronto for Ogdensburg, N.Y. Later than 8:00 P.M. I again returned to the house where the children were imprisoned, and ended their lives by connecting the gas with the trunk. Then came the opening of the trunk and the viewing of their little blackened and distorted faces, then the digging of their shallow graves in the basement of the house, the ruthless stripping off of their clothing, and the burial without a particle of covering save the cold earth, which I heaped upon them with fiendish delight."

* * *

"Ten years ago," Holmes wrote at the opening of his confession, "I was thoroughly examined by four men of marked ability and by them pronounced as being both mentally and physically a normal and healthy man. To-day I have every attribute of a degenerate—a moral idiot. Is it possible that the crimes, instead of being the result of these abnormal conditions, are in themselves the occasion of the degeneracy?"

Holmes followed this enticing question with an account of what he saw as ominous changes in his physical appearance while incarcerated at Moyamensing—with some additional commentary that gives us a glimpse of the primitive state of the science of criminology in 1896.

183

"Even at the time of my arrest in 1894," he explained, "no defects were noticeable under the searching Bertillon system of measurements to which I was subjected, but later, and more noticeably within the past few months, these defects have increased with startling rapidity, as is made known to me by each succeeding examination until I have become thankful that I am no longer allowed a glass with which to note my rapidly deteriorating condition. . . ."

And what exactly were those physical abnormalities?

"The principal defects that have thus far developed and which are all established signs of degeneracy, are a decided prominence upon one side of my head and a corresponding diminution upon the other side; a marked deficiency of one side of my nose and of one ear, together with an abnormal increase of each upon the opposite side; a difference of one and one-half inches in the length of my arms and an equal shortening of one leg from knee to heel; also a most malevolent distortion of one side of my face and of one eye—so marked and terrible that in writing of it for publication, Hall Caine, although I wore a beard at the time to conceal it as best I could, described that side of my face as marked by a deep line of crime and being that of a devil—so apparent that an expert criminologist in the employ of the United States Government who had never previously seen me said within thirty seconds after entering my cell: 'I know you are guilty.' "

If Holmes needed any further proof of his rapidly escalating degeneracy, he found it in his heartless murder of young Howard Pitezel. "If I could now recall one circumstance," he concluded, "a dollar of money to be gained, a disagreeable act or word upon his part, in justification of this horrid crime, it would be a satisfaction to me; but to think that I committed this and other crimes for the pleasure of killing my fellow beings, to hear their cries for mercy and pleas to be allowed even sufficient time to pray and prepare for death—all this is now too horrible for even me, hardened criminal that I am, to again live over without a shudder. Is it to be wondered at that since my arrest my days have been those of self-reproaching torture, and my nights of sleepless fear? Or that even before my death, I have commenced to assume the form and features of the Evil One himself?"

10
HOLMES' CAREER OVER

Homicidal Monster Is Hanged in
the Moyamensing Prison.

TAKES FIFTEEN ·MINUTES TO DIE

His Wonderful Nerve Stays with
Him on the Scaffold.

BODY IS BURIED IN CEMENT

Strange Coincidences Lead to
Talk of an "Astral" Holmes.

THE AMAZING HOLMES:
MAN OR MONSTER?

When the priests left Holmes' cell the night before his execution, he was weak and tearful. In the light of later events it is apparent, though, that his condition was the result of the many tensions of the day, rather than of a general breakdown. The only man who remained with him was Keeper George Weaver, the night watch, who asked the condemned man if he cared to go to sleep, receiving a soft-spoken yes in reply. Holmes undressed slowly and almost painfully, saying very little and taking little interest in conversation with his guard.

"I don't know where I'll sleep tomorrow night," he said, when he had gone through his brief devotions and stretched himself on the couch. "But nobody knows that."

Holmes turned his back against the light that was burning just beneath the open door of his cell, and almost immediately fell asleep. He moved only once or twice during the next six hours and did not awaken at any time. The guard looked at the resting figure, the piles of paper neatly folded on the small table, the picture of a woman on the wall, the crucifix above the bed, the folded clothes that would soon be a shroud, and the well-worn slippers on the floor, which were never to be worn again. He had come to know Holmes better than anyone else, and he was heavyhearted.

When the prison clock struck six, Keeper John Henry, the day watch, came down the corridor to reliever Weaver, and the two awakened Holmes. They called him twice and then shook him with considerable vigor before his eyes opened and his final night's sleep on earth ended. He sat up and greeted them almost cheerily.

"Good morning," he said, "is it six o'clock already?"

H. H. Holmes in jail. From the *Chicago Times-Herald*, July 21, 1895, p. 2.

"Yes," replied Henry, "how do you feel?"

"First-rate. I was very tired last night and was glad to get to bed. I never slept better in my life."

Holmes made some inquiries about trivial matters, and shaved as unconcernedly as a man might do who expected to follow the routine a thousand more times before he died. The thought that he was now doing everything for the last time did not seem to affect him at all, and he ordered a substantial breakfast. He then began to dress. Contrary to the general custom, he refused to don a new suit but arrayed himself in trousers, vest, and cutaway coat of some pepper-and-salt effect that had been worn by him frequently before. Even in this he was careful, giving every attention to the most minute details of his dress.

Weaver left and Henry took the guard seat at the door, Holmes resuming work at the innumerable letters that he felt called upon to write before his execution. They were addressed to the women he had married, to most of his relatives, and even to the friends of some of his victims. He wrote out, too, the instructions to his lawyers regarding disposition of his entangled estate.

The minutes passed rapidly. Rev. P. J. Dailey and his assistant, Rev. Henry J. McPake, of the Church of the Annunciation, came into the cell and were warmly greeted by Holmes. After communion he finished his breakfast, and they remarked that his appetite had not failed him.

Breakfast was followed almost immediately by the arrival of attorney Samuel P. Rotan. The young lawyer glanced anxiously into Holmes' face, and when he saw it light up with a smile of welcome, his own brightened.

"You're all right," he said. "You look lots better than you did last night."

In reply Holmes held out his left arm with the fingers of the hand separated and said, "See if I tremble."

There was no tremor noticeable, although the guard looked too, and Holmes and his lawyer almost immediately fell into a lengthy and earnest conversation. It concerned the packing of the body, after the execution, in cement, a plan devised by Holmes during the long days that he had spent in prison waiting for death. Rotan told him that only the day before he had been offered $5,000 for Holmes' corpse and had put the man who made the proposition out of his office.

"Thank you," said Holmes quietly. "I'll see that no one gets my body, either by buying it or stealing it." Perhaps he was thinking of his own body-snatching escapades, or of the medical scientists who wanted to examine his brain in search of any abnormalities that might explain his life of crime.

When the breakfast dishes were removed, Holmes wrote a few words on a piece of paper and handed it to Rotan with the remark that he would never touch pen to paper again. The words were a brief, sincere tribute of personal affection and gratitude for all that the attorney had done for him. Holmes then turned himself over entirely to the priests, and from that time on until the drop fell they were always with him. He entered into the ceremonies of the fearful occasion with a solemn face but did not for a moment show signs of depression or fear.

While Holmes was on his knees in his tiny cell saying his final prayers over and over again, there was businesslike activity in the offices and reception room of the prison. Fifty-one people had been invited by Sheriff Clement to witness the execution and they had all arrived by nine o'clock, many of them coming in carriages and leaving a row of vehicles in front of the gray building that helped attract a crowd. Those who held tickets of admission were forced to fight their way through this crowd, occasionally having to call in the assistance of a policeman.

On the inside there was dampness in the air and the smell of a prison. The witnesses moved restlessly about from the stone roadway in the center of the main entrance to the reception room, which opened from it, asking each other if they had ever seen a hanging before. Most of them had not. The guests were a curious mixture of youth and old age, the cub reporter on his first assignment to a hanging rubbing elbows with the gray-haired physician who had seen more executions than he had time to talk about just then. Among them were the president of Fidelity Mutual, L. G. Fouse, and Detective Frank Geyer.

Sheriff Clement was indignant when he discovered that some of the prison inspectors had taken advantage of their official position to bring in between twenty-five and thirty of their personal friends, who mingled freely with the other guests. He threatened to eject the outsiders but abandoned the idea because of the lateness of the hour.

Meanwhile, the throng of morbidly curious spectators had grown outside the prison. Some had arrived as early as half-past seven. A ghostly silence predominated that was broken only occasionally by the clang of an electric car bell or the rattle of a wagon's wheels. The multitude itself was painfully silent, waiting for the signal from within the prison walls announcing that Holmes had paid the supreme penalty for his crimes.

* * *

The twelve men constituting the sheriff's jury were called together in the reception room and lined up before a long table, where they were addressed by Assistant Solicitor Grew. He explained their duties and administered the oath that bound them to report truthfully the cause of the death they were about to witness. They all took the oath and signed the pledge. It was a curious coincidence that one of them, a Germantown yarn manufacturer named Samuel Wood, had also been a member of the jury that tried and convicted Holmes.

A long wait followed the swearing in of the jury, during which the nervousness of most of the witnesses perceptibly increased. Superintendent Perkins and his assistants made mysterious visits to the gallows and to Holmes' cell, both of which were in the long corridor running north from the reception room. When the door leading into this corridor opened and closed, a glimpse could be caught of the scaffold.

At ten o'clock sharp the jury was asked to fall in line, and the others rushed for a favorable position behind them. The door was opened, and the long procession of men with bared heads and grave faces walked down a short flight of steps and across the asphalt pavement, past what seemed like endless rows of cells. Holmes was in one of them, waiting, listening to the steady tramp of the men who had come to see him die.

The scaffold reached entirely across the corridor, with a door on one side permitting the witnesses to pass through to its front. When the last man had crossed the threshold of this door, it was closed, shutting off all outside observation. Almost at that instant the door of Holmes' cell opened and he stepped out between the two priests, followed by Assistant Superintendent Richardson and lawyer Rotan. Holmes had demanded the presence of Rotan on the scaffold, and Sheriff Clement had given a reluctant consent.

Superintendent Perkins and the sheriff walked arm in arm up the thirteen steps that led to the scaffold, and behind them came the priests chanting the Miserere, their white robes making even that scene look picturesque. Holmes, when he reached the scaffold, held a crucifix in his hand and continued praying until the priests stopped. Then he opened his eyes, lifted his head, and

191

walked to the edge of the scaffold, confronting the white faces of the crowd below. Between him and this crowd was a semicircle of uniformed guards. A rail reaching to his waist ran around the edge of the scaffold, and on this he rested his hands as calmly as if he were himself a spectator and the rest of the little party a show.

There was something pitiable in the picture of the man as he stood looking down upon his audience. His slender frame was clothed in a loose-fitting suit and above the cutaway coat appeared a white handkerchief loosely tied about his throat. His brown moustache and hair had been recently trimmed, but it cannot be said that he presented a good appearance. The prison pallor on his face gave one a chill. He looked dead already.

When he had surveyed the crowd, Holmes began to talk, and his tones were as steady and smooth as those of an orator making an after-dinner speech. He made no gestures, but emphasized words on occasion. Everything he said was plainly audible. No one else in the crowd could have kept as steady a voice.

"Gentlemen," he began, "I have very few words to say. In fact, I would make no remarks at this time were it not for the feeling that if I did not speak it would imply that I acquiesced in my execution. I only wish to say that the extent of the wrongdoing I am guilty of in taking human life is the killing of two women. They died by my hands as the results of criminal operations.

"I wish also to state," he continued, "so that no chance of misunderstanding may exist hereafter, that I am not guilty of taking the lives of any of the Pitezel family, either the three children or the father, Benjamin F. Pitezel, for whose death I am now to be hanged. I have never committed murder. That is all I have to say."

As he spoke the last sentence he turned half around and put his right hand on Rotan's broad shoulder. Holmes smiled as he said, "Good-bye, Sam. You have done all you could." He whispered a few other words and then hugged the young attorney, who almost ran down the scaffold steps when he was released.

The priests motioned to the condemned man to kneel, and he did so, still grasping the little crucifix in his hands. For two minutes his lips moved in silent prayer, and he arose steadily to his feet when he had finished. He shook hands with the greatest heartiness with Fathers Dailey and McPake, carefully buttoned his coat, then nodded to the prison officials.

As the priests resumed their chant, Richardson stepped forward, and drawing Holmes' hands behind him dexterously handcuffed him. The man stood as straight and steady as one of the black beams beside him, looking quietly upon the last human faces he was ever to see. Sheriff Clement and Superintendent Perkins left the scaffold and Richardson drew the black cap down over Holmes' face. "Take your time about it," Holmes remarked. "You know I am in no hurry."

His advice was not heeded. Richardson unwound the rope from about the beam, ran out the noose, and slipped it over Holmes' head. As he drew it tight about the neck there came in muffled, but steady, tones, "Good-bye—good-bye, everybody."

Richardson stepped back and dropped a handkerchief. At exactly 10:12½ the black boards on which Holmes stood parted in the middle, and down through the opening his body fell, stopping with a jerk that knocked his head to one side and sent his legs swinging far out toward the spectators. The contortions lasted for a minute, the body turning round and round and the legs swaying backwards and forwards as if the man were struggling to break the merciless rope. The back and chest heaved, the fingers opened and closed repeatedly, and there were twitchings about the exposed neck.

From this ghastly spectacle most of the guests turned to look at the whitewashed walls. Two of them fainted and one fell, but was quickly brought to his feet. The dangling body slowly but surely settled at the end of the rope, and gradually all movement ceased. Doctors Butcher and Sharp felt the pulse and put their ears over the heart. For fifteen minutes they listened for heart beats, and at the end of that time they pronounced him dead.

The crowd of spectators began wandering around the corridor, and most of them were relieved to know that the body would not be lowered until it had hung for another quarter of an hour. After life was extinct, Lieutenant Tomlinson was permitted to bring in his sergeants and patrolmen and they marched in line by the scaffold, each one critically surveying the corpse. It was about the strangest reception that man could imagine, and it made some shudder to hear the comments. The policemen seemed to enjoy the sight.

When the delay began to seem intolerably long, Dr. Butcher gave permission to lower the body, and it was let down onto a truck very much like a bag of potatoes would be thrown about. The officials had a very hard time with the rope. The noose had sunk deep into the flesh and did not easily become separated, and Superintendent Perkins refused to have it cut off, although Rotan begged him to do so. After several minutes of struggling, the job was accomplished and the black cap taken off.

The dead man's face was a thing too ghastly for description, and even the doctors turned from it. An examination of the neck showed that the axis had been separated from the atlas by the fall—in other words, the neck was broken. No autopsy was performed, and Rotan stood guard to see that Holmes' wishes in this respect were obeyed. While standing there he was asked what the contents of the papers were that Holmes had turned over to him.

"I have not gone over them yet," he replied, "but I understand that they are mostly directions to his attorneys to keep up the effort to prove his innocence of murder."

"Does he want that effort kept up?"

"He does, and he believes it will one day be successful. So do I."

"Did he leave any money with which to prosecute a search?"

"He did not leave any with me—not one cent."

At this point the arrival of the undertaker's wagon caught Rotan's attention, and he checked the transfer of the corpse. As the wagon drove out through the tremendous crowd awaiting it at the west gate, the young attorney followed it into the street.

Soon the crowd of witnesses to the hanging began to thin out. They left the prison one by one, facing all manner of questions when they passed through the mob waiting at the gate, and giving thanks for the privilege of breathing the free air and seeing the sun once again. Assistant Superintendent Richardson was frequently congratulated on the success of the execution—as if the outcome had ever been in doubt—and in reply he said just as frequently that Holmes was the nerviest of the sixty-seven men he had seen die. Superintendent Perkins agreed, and so did the physicians.

* * *

Unique in life, Holmes would be unique in the grave. Attorney Rotan made certain that the interment followed the expressed wishes of Holmes in every detail.

It was a few minutes before noon when undertaker J. J. O'Rourke, whose office was at the corner of Tenth and Tasker streets, drove to Moyamensing Prison with his undertaker's wagon. In it was an ordinary pine box, in which the body was placed. O'Rourke then drove out of the Reed Street entrance to the prison and hurried back to the rear yard of his residence. There he had a larger box and five barrels of cement and sand. He and his assistants quickly mixed the mortar and placed a layer perhaps ten inches deep in the box, which was first placed in the wagon that would haul it to the cemetery. Holmes' body was placed on top of this bed of cement, attired as he was when he dropped through the trap.

A silk handkerchief was spread over his face and then more mortar piled into the box. It was packed tightly around the lifeless form and soon covered the still features. As two Pinkerton detectives, engaged to watch the body, looked on, still more mortar was thrown into the box until it was full. The lid was then nailed down and the wagon started away for Holy Cross Cemetery in Delaware County.

It was nearly two o'clock when the undertaker's wagon reached the cemetery. The superintendent, R. B. Campbell, refused to allow the body to be placed in the vault without special instructions from Joseph F. Haley, a clerk in the cathedral, back in Philadelphia. There was nothing to do but dispatch a man to secure the permit from Mr. Haley. After a tedious wait of three hours, the messenger returned and preparations were made for removing the box and its heavy contents to the vault. It was a comparatively easy task to pull the box out of the wagon and let it drop onto the ground. To move it after it was on terra firma was another matter.

O'Rourke, his two assistants, the two detectives, and a couple of cemetery employees took hold and lifted, but the box did not move. Again they heaved and strained and succeeded in breaking the handles, but again the hardened cement refused to budge. The men were in a quandary. They had never had such a task before and they regretted that they did not have a block and tackle, such as is used for moving safes.

195

Finally a group of reporters who had been watching the proceedings came to the assistance of the men. Thirteen pairs of stout arms seized the corners of the box, and by dint of shoving and pulling moved it inch by inch into the vault. Once the box was there, the vault was closed, and the group of tired and perspiring workers all left the cemetery except the detectives. They remained all night, keeping a lonely vigil over the vault until the body could be quietly and privately buried the following day in a grave ten feet deep, with a two-foot layer of cement on top of the coffin.

As soon as he was notified that the execution had taken place, undertaker O'Rourke filed a return of death with the Board of Health. This was recorded by Registry Clerk Theodore M. Carr, and in deference to the notoriety of the deceased he made the record with red ink. The certificate of death, which was signed by Benjamin F. Butcher, M.D., gave the name of the deceased as Herman W. Mudgett, alias H. H. Holmes, and further described him as white, male, thirty-five years old, and married. The cause of death was stated as "hanging according to law." O'Rourke in his certificate did not give any occupation for Holmes, and listed his place of birth as the United States, omitting any mention of tiny Gilmanton, New Hampshire.

*   *   *

For almost everyone the hanging of Holmes was the final and certain end of a bizarre and exciting career of crime. But for a few others, there were too many sinister and seemingly related events before and after the execution to make it that simple. Talk began of an "evil eye" and of an "astral" quality in Holmes.

During Holmes' trial great attention had been given to a horoscope of the murderer implying that any persons connected with him, and especially with his conviction and death, would meet with misfortune and possibly their own demise. The combinations of the planets at his birth denoted many changes in life, much mystery, extraordinary conduct, a fanciful, emotional temperament, and a most fickle character. The next succeeding signs showed infallible tokens of disaster, foreshadowing failure in business enterprise and the casting of misfortune on others. His final signs could be interpreted only to mean death by judge and jury.

The horoscope's intimation of disaster for persons associated with Holmes was not treated too seriously until a chain of personal misfortunes began to unfold. Soon there was talk of "something magnetically evil about the man whose murders have shocked the world," and of "an influence malignant in the extreme, and which not only pervades the very atmosphere about him, but, so it would seem, has actually the telepathic property of transmission. . . ."

To begin with, there was the death from blood poisoning of Dr. William K. Mattern, who, as coroner's physician, was an important witness against Holmes.

Then there was the dangerous illness of Coroner Ashbridge, who held the inquest upon the body found in the Callowhill Street house, an illness that at one time caused friends to despair of his life.

There followed the illness of Judge Arnold, who tried and sentenced Holmes, and who for a time also hovered on the very brink of death.

There was the suicide of Superintendent Perkins of Moyamensing Prison, in which the murderer had been confined.

There was the death of Holmes' lawyer in Chicago.

There was the fate of Peter Cigrand, father of Emeline, who pleaded with Holmes to tell him the truth about his daughter's death, and who was horribly burned in a gas explosion as he prepared to go to Philadelphia to see Holmes, and, if possible, witness the hanging.

And there was the professional misfortune, ending in disbarment, that awaited William A. Shoemaker, the young attorney who first defended Holmes.

But it was the death of one of the priests who had attended Holmes at the hanging, a fire in the Fidelity Mutual building, and, above all, the violent end of the jury foreman that most forcefully captured the imagination of the superstitious.

When the body of Rev. Henry J. McPake was found in the rear yard of a church, Dr. Cattell, the new coroner's physician, named uremia as the cause of death. This was merely saying that death

197

was due to natural causes. "There was no fracture of the skull; no hemorrhage," said the doctor. "He had typhoid fever last winter. His injuries were superficial, and no more than could be gotten from a fall." Without hesitation, the police accepted Cattell's verdict as the solution to the mystery of the priest's death.

But, it was asked, why was the doctor so positive that the priest fell where he was found?

Do men who die of uremia usually seek backyards and dark alleyways after midnight when they feel death approaching?

Does uremia produce marks of violence about the head?

Does uremia spirit watches and other valuables from a man's pockets?

Does uremia result in the disarrangement of a man's clothing?

Would uremia produce bloodstains on the fence and the marks of boot heels near the body?

If not, it was said, then something more than uremia killed Father McPake.

As for the fire, it took place in the office of O. LeForrest Perry, the supervisor of city agents for the Fidelity Mutual Life Insurance Company who was instrumental in the arrest of Holmes. The fire began in his office and was extinguished before it affected the rest of the company's building, but Perry's entire office was in ruins. His desk was burned up, together with several checks and some valuable papers, and the carpet was beyond repair. All was a shambles—all, that is, except the warrant for the arrest of Holmes that hung over his desk in a frame, with two cabinet photographs of the dead man. The frame enclosing it was burned up, the glass was cracked in several places by the heat, but the warrant itself was undamaged except for slight discoloration in spots.

Mr. Perry's clerks declared that it was a Jonah, and wanted it thrown away.

According to the superstitious, the jury foreman, Linford L. Biles, became a "marked man" before he even heard of Holmes. Biles' house stood ominously in the shadow of a cemetery, and there was repeated trouble from the occasional contact of a live telephone wire with a telegraph wire over his roof. Nothing much was thought of the sparks that resulted when a heavy wind or storm brought the wires together, until one Saturday afternoon when a fire resulted and had to be extinguished. That was the very afternoon that Holmes was arrested in Boston. And Biles was fated to be the foreman of the jury that would try and convict the "alleged insurance swindler."

After Holmes' execution, history repeated itself for Linford Biles and he awoke one morning to learn of another fire on his roof. In a few minutes he was on top of the house, attempting to hack away the wire that was causing the blaze. A crowd of neighbors watching from the street heard a heavy thud, like the fall of a body, and then silence. Biles was dead, having apparently received a shock that was sufficient to kill a dozen men. His left hand was scorched, the forehead was discolored, and there was a scar on one foot. He must have walked unexpectedly on the end of the live wire, with the wet roof also acting as a conductor to the charge that killed him.

* * *

The timing of the first fire, the way in which Biles died, the warnings of Holmes' horoscope—could these all be mere coincidences? There were more than enough such "coincidences" to feed the rumor mills of the chart readers for years. Yet, even among those who considered themselves scientific and advanced in their thought, there were attempts to explain Holmes' prodigious career of crime in terms of some mysterious and monstrous physical abnormality. The concept of a loving, considerate man and a bloodthirsty monster inhabiting the same physical frame was apparently too much to accept—perhaps partly out of fear of its implications for the rest of us "human" beings.

One thing Holmes had accomplished, whether intentionally or not, was to earn himself a reputation as the most fiendish killer in the annals of American crime. His descriptions in the public press had escalated from "that prince of insurance swindlers" to the "king of fabricators" and finally "the versatile butcher." The Chicago *Times-Herald* found that "to parallel such a career one must go back to past ages and to the time of the Borgias or Brinvilliers, and even these were not such human monsters as

199

Holmes seems to have been. He is a prodigy of wickedness, a human demon, a being so unthinkable to the mind that no novelist would dare to invent such a character. The story, too, tends to illustrate the end of the century."

Like the Borgias to whom he was so often compared, Holmes did at least have style. Indeed, W. H. Williamson, writing during the Roaring Twenties of the current century and looking back with nostalgia to the Holmes era, would lament that "today Chicago's criminals, of whom the world knows, are raw, rough, even uncouth. They are coarse workers with whom the old timers would have been ashamed to associate. Instead of brains, they use force. Instead of cunning, they use machine guns."

His seductive style, nevertheless, was scarcely appreciated by Holmes' victims once they discerned its true purpose, and as he was removed from the gallows the *New York Times* would reflect that "it takes a very convinced opponent of capital punishment to maintain that any better disposition could have been made of the wretch Holmes." Undoubtedly the *Inter Ocean* spoke for most people when it said that "a sigh of relief will go up from the whole country with the knowledge that Herman Mudgett, or Henry H. Holmes, man or monster, has been exterminated—much the same as a plague to humanity would be stamped out."

Man or monster, indeed. Perhaps both?

APPENDIXES

APPENDIXES

APPENDIX ONE
Holmes' Englewood

When we reflect on the energy misspent by Holmes on his dubious enterprises, we can only imagine what wonders he might have accomplished had character and self-discipline tamed the ingenuity within him. He possessed the quick wit, winning personality, and creative turn of mind that could have propelled him into the front ranks of Chicago's favorite sons had he chosen, let us say, politics or legitimate commerce as his profession. There are indications, too, that his business sense was first-rate when not deformed by the need for some easy money. His selection of Englewood as his home base proves that.

Englewood was first known as The Junction or Junction Grove, for it was the junction of three railroad routes that brought the first settlers to the area. Around 1868, when the population consisted of less than twenty families, the name was changed to Englewood—a name derived, ironically, from the home of the ancient outlaws Adam Bell, "Clym of the Clough," and William Cloudsley. These noted predecessors of Robin Hood and his merry men made their home in the forests of Englewood, near Carlisle, in England. It was a fitting namesake for the young Illinois settlement, which at that time was a forest of luxuriant oak trees.

Englewood began to lose its provincial character when the great fire of 1871 swept Chicago. There was a rush for homes in outlying areas, and Englewood's population increased rapidly. By 1882 the *Englewood Directory* could boast that "hers is the best locality for suburban residence in the vicinity of Chicago. She enjoys advantages as an accessible point which none of her sister suburbs can claim. Seven leading lines of railway furnish forty-five trains each way daily, and within three months two more railroads and a line of street cars will be added. *All* of these trains *must* stop at Englewood. These magnificent facilities give us advantages possessed by no other suburb of Chicago, the majority of which are mere flag stations, dependent upon one or two dummy trains a day, while the regular trains whizz through the town unmindful of its interests." Nor were its advantages limited to a commuter train schedule that would be the envy of today's suburbs. "Located twelve feet above the level of the lake, with a perfect water, sewerage and gas system, and an excellent police and fire department, Englewood combines all of the conveniences of the city, with the fresh, healthful air of the country. . . . We have more enterprising men and less 'dead-beats' than any other suburb in the country."

This apparently was more than mere chamber of commerce puffery. In 1879 the *Englewood Directory* contained 1,100 names, and in 1882 about 1,800 residents were noted. During the eighties the population exploded so rapidly that by 1890 it exceeded 45,000, and Chicago guides lamented that Englewood "is practically within the old city, and has long since lost its individuality as a village." Irish, German, and older residents, fleeing the inner city of Chicago, gave it a cosmopolitan and middle-class flavor. Additions and subdivisions were laid out, with maple and elm trees planted along the street lines (the early settlers had long since destroyed the original oaks). While most of the new homes were modest frame or brick structures, land was still cheap enough to induce the wealthy to build pretentious mansions, particularly along Harvard, Yale, Ross, and Wentworth avenues. Waterworks, gasworks, and other city conveniences made their appearance and in 1889 Englewood was formally annexed by Chicago, along with the city of Lake View and the towns of Lake, Hyde Park, Jefferson, and Cicero.

Holmes chose well, therefore, when he selected Englewood as his home. An ambitious businessman could hardly fail in the growing, fashionable suburb, with its prosperous middle-class trade. But Holmes' acute eye led him not merely to the right neighborhood, but to the very intersection destined to become the center of its business life. Vacant land was still available at Sixty-third and Wallace streets when he bought a corner lot and constructed his bizarre Castle. A few years later, however, the scene was changed beyond recognition. As a neighborhood newspaper would later recall, "Merchants doing business during the '90s on Sixty-third Street were nerveless men if one considers the daily din they put up with. Nucleus of the local business world was located near Wallace Street where the Western Indiana railroad crossed the thoroughfare at street level. Chugging engines tooted whistles, clanged bells and sighed with escaping steam as they stopped and started at the station." Had Holmes been more circumspect in his morals and his business dealings, a tidy fortune would have resulted from his real estate investment. He undoubtedly would have lived to see electricity introduced to Englewood in 1897, and three years later he could have confronted the face of the future at Chicago's first automobile show. As late as 1923 a local historian could report that "Sixty-third Street is acknowledged to be the most prosperous and best developed cross street in the great city of Chicago."

For Holmes that was not to be, but the years he did live in Englewood were colorful and exciting ones. Just a couple of miles east, Americans were witnessing the dawn of technology at the great World's Columbian Exposition. Englewood was more than familiar with the steam railroads that constituted the nervous system of the nation's economy, for they now made more than one hundred stops a day at its stations, and downtown Chicago was constructing elevated railroad tracks for commuter trains of three or four cars pulled by small locomotives burning anthracite coal. Locally, however, the horse would remain the beast of transportation for at least a few more years. The seasonal rains of the spring brought a common sight: horses mired to the belly in mud, and the loaded wagons they were drawing almost out of sight in the gummy earth. Plodding horses also brought streetcars to Englewood in 1892, with the first line running in front of Holmes' Castle along Sixty-third Street. It took about fifteen minutes to go a mile, but there was straw on the floor of the cars to keep your feet warm in the winter, and if the tracks were blocked, the crew would simply derail the car and continue forging ahead.

The railroad tracks adjacent to Wallace Street posed a special problem. Two white horses, hitched together as a team, stood at the intersection of the street and the tracks all day long. When a horse-drawn streetcar approached, the white horses whinnied and walked out into the tracks. The streetcar driver would leave the front platform, pick up the lines, and hitch them to the harness of the permanent horse. All three would strain under the shout, "Giddyup!" and pull the car over the tracks. Reaching the other side, the team would be unhitched and left waiting for another car coming from the opposite direction.

Gaslights began to line Englewood streets in 1881. Each of the lamps was mounted on a cast-iron pole ten feet high, and had to be lit individually by a lamplighter. His equipment consisted of a small ladder, a pole with an indented top in which a match could be inserted, and usually a bicycle. Soon the pole and matches were replaced by a blowtorch.

As notorious as Holmes' Castle later became, it could not match the style of Englewood's most imposing edifice, the Timmerman Opera House. Located four blocks east of Holmes, on Sixty-third at the corner of Stewart Avenue, its construction had cost the then princely sum of $100,000, and *The Standard Guide to Chicago for the Year 1891* reported that "the building is finished in red brick, terra cotta and stone trimmings, and is exceedingly pleasing in architectural design. There are large bay windows on the Sixty-third Street front and handsome iron balconies on the Stewart Avenue side. The auditorium is on the ground floor, and in beauty and richness of furnishings and decorations is equal to any theatre in the city. Silk, velvet and plush draperies in harmonious shades add to the elegance of the luxurious interior. The aisles are wide and the seat rows are arranged with sufficient width between to insure the comfort of auditors. Twelve hundred persons may find seats—the first floor and balcony being provided with opera chairs—and several hundred others may see the stage from 'standing room,' should they so elect. The house is lighted by incandescent electric lights and is heated by steam, a late device in ventilation being employed. The precautions against danger from fire are most complete. The theatre is open on four sides, and in addition to this there are seven exits from the main floor, six from the balcony and three from the gallery. It is calculated that when the house is crowded the audience may disperse in one and one-half minutes. The stage is forty-nine feet wide and thirty-four feet deep, while the height to the rigging loft is ninety feet. A complete and modern stage equipment has been given the stage, and the most pretentious productions may be perfectly presented on its boards. The drop curtain, the work of a local artist, presents a handsome marine view."

Adjacent to the Timmerman Opera House was another magnificent structure, the New Julien Hotel, with a reputation as the finest furnished family hotel on the South Side. It opened in 1890 with seventy-six spacious and pleasantly furnished suites.

Financial & Commercial Chicago, a directory of Chicagoland businesses and businessmen published in 1891, gives us laudatory glimpses of a few of Holmes' neighbors. Across the street at 700 Sixty-third—which, in fact, must have been the building that at one time housed Mrs. Holton's pharmacy—was A. A. Frazier, a Scottish-born architect who enjoyed a wide patronage among builders and substantial property owners. One or two doors down, at number 706, was the South Side Printing House. John P. Honeycutt, its owner, was a printer and pressman from Tennessee who had left Rand & McNally to establish his own business. And on the same block, at number 726, was the firm of Young & Clark, engaged in real estate, insurance, loans, and renting. J. W. Young was a Chicago lawyer and George Clark an Englishman who possessed "in an eminent degree those qualities of business tact and shrewdness, combined with a pleasant and agreeable manner which qualify the successful commercial man."

Another Englishman could be found at Sixty-third and Halstead. There Charles W. Fenn conducted his work as a broker in real estate, catering to a conservative patronage. *Financial & Commercial Chicago* advised its readers that "in addition to his business qualifications Mr. Fenn is also a gifted musician of more than ordinary ability, ranking among the finest soloists. This, together with his geniality and courteous manners, make him a social favourite, while his conservative policy in business has gained him the confidence of a large patronage."

Finally, in Holmes' Castle at 703 Sixty-third, the guide placed the offices of commission merchants Gregson & Fischer. George Gregson ran the firm's large downtown office, with H. F. Fischer the partner in charge of the newer Englewood branch. "They handle all kinds of farm produce, paying particular attention to butter, eggs and poultry. Daily market reports sent to patrons on application. The firm is regarded as one of the most reliable and trustworthy ones with men of known worth at its head. The Prairie State National Bank is offered as a reference as to their trading."

In January 1975 several friends and I made a pilgrimage to the site of Holmes' Castle and found a scene of quiet desolation. Englewood now rests in the midst of Chicago's vast slums, and boarded-up, decaying houses and sterile public housing projects have replaced the opera house and streetcars and bustling traffic of Sixty-third Street, reminding me of those somber engravings portraying Civil War destruction. Weeds and junk mark the site where Emeline Cigrand and Julia Conner and unknown numbers of others met their fate. The Castle is gone now, but Englewood lives under the siege of a different and far more pervasive horror.

* * *

H. H. Holmes' public career in the suburban Chicago neighborhood of Englewood can be traced dramatically through listings in the city directories as reproduced on the following pages.

Left margin (vertical text): Wentworth Ave. 5102 CO. SAVINGS & LOAN SIDE PARK in Stock Lake

DRESSMAKERS—CONTINUED.

Preston Sadie I. es State 2d s 61st, Englewood
Putnam Lottie Miss, 635 Gordon
Rhoades B. C. Mrs. 5564 Atlantic, Englewood
Scott Cora A. Miss, es Winter 1st s 68th, Normal Park
Steel William Mrs. 548 Duncan Park
Sterrit Maggie Miss, 716, 47th
Stoller Minnie Miss, 4351 Butterfield
Stowe M. Mrs. 6242 Wentworth av, Englewood
STRICKLAND JULIA MRS. 426, 61st
Sweetman Maggie Miss, 4161 Wentworth av
Toliaferro Mrs. T. T. ns of 65th 1st e Halsted, Englewood
Troy J. C. Mrs. 4829 Justine
Wade Phœbe C. Mrs. 755 Gordon
Walker E. Mrs. 423, 59th, Englewood
WENNERSKOLD C. A. MRS. 5238 Wentworth
     av (see adv p. III)
Yerty M. D. Miss, 6435 Wentworth av

DRUGGISTS.

BARNES JOHN, 825, 43d
Bell John I. 4700 State
BONHEIM FRANK, 4358 State
BONHEIM LEE M. 5421 Wentworth av
CALDWELL PETER, 711, 43d
CORY V. P & CO. 4101 State
DIETZ JOHN, 3905 Wentworth av
HOGAN & HISGEN, 6214 Wentworth av, Englewood
HOLTON E. S. 63d cor Wallace, Englewood
HOUGHTON H. J. 6560 Wentworth av, Englewood
HURST N. N. 5100 Wentworth av and 3906 State
HURST'S PHARMACIES, 5100 Wentworth av and
     3906 State
Justi W. F. 4644 Wentworth av
KOTZENBERG CHARLES, 4203 S. Halsted
Masquelet John, 47th cor Bishop
Mehl William, 4658 Ashland av
NORTH CHARLES F. Tillotson Block, Englewood
PIERPOINT BROS. ws Lincoln av 2d n of 68th,
     Englewood
PORTER M. N. & CO. State cor 39th and Indiana
     av cor 39th
REASNER & CO. 5727 Wentworth av, Englewood
Ritter A. Paul, 4341 Halsted
Sandmeyer Henry, 736, 43d

In 1886 Holmes takes a position in the drug store of the widow E. S. Holton.
The *Town of Lake Directory, 1886*, gives this listing for Mrs. Holton, and con-
tains no mention of Holmes. Courtesy of the Chicago Historical Society.

The very next year, it is Mrs. Holton who is missing from the *Town of Lake Directory, 1887*—and from the community as well—while Holmes has this advertisement (second from the top of the page) for his drugs and other products. Courtesy of the Chicago Historical Society.

G. J. THOMPSON & CO. | Merchant Tailors, 311 63d St., ENGLEWOOD.

Holding Charles W. purchasing agt. 188 South Water, r 6230 Princeton av
Holding Melville G. salesman 207 Randolph, r 441, 67th
Holick Edward, r 5617 Butterfield
Holland John switchman r 5615 Green
Holland John G. clerk bds. 430 Cedar
Holland M. C. janitor 313, 63d
Holland Timothy C. agent r 433, 58th
Hollecker G. D. salesman J. V. Farwell & Co. r 416 Cedar
Hollenback Wesley, blacksmith r 319 Cedar
Hollenbeck R. E. carpenter r 445 Maple
Hollenbeck William A. clerk r 5636 Wentworth av
Hollett R. P. lawyer 162 Washington r 6535 Stewart av
Hollie James W. police r 5504 State
Hollihan Jesse, laborer r 5524 Dearborn
Hollingsworth Charlotte Mrs. 7030 Stewart av
Hollingsworth Harry A. clerk r 7030 Stewart av
Hollingsworth James, machinist r 7030 Stewart av
Hollister A. N. driver r 6108 State
Hollister Walter, switchman r 6500 Wentworth av
Hollowed Patrick, conductor r 6721 Peoria
Hollst Edward, mattressmkr. r es Winter 8th n 81st, Auburn Pk
Holm August, tailor r 771, 64th
Holm Augusta, domestic 6704 Stewart av
Holm Gus, carpenter r 1250, 63d
Holm Nels, painter 5932 May
Holm Oscar, carpenter bds. 6607 Peoria
HOLMAN E. E. physician 63d and Stewart av, r The New Julien Hotel
Holman H. W. claim clerk C. & E. I. R. R. 537, 67th
Holman W. E. lather bds. 6357 Yale
Holmen Albert, delivery clerk r 6106 Wright
Holmes Carrie L. stenographer r 6389 Dickey
Holmes Chas. switchman bds. 83d cor Vincennes av, Auburn Pk
Holmes C. O. contractor and builder 6359 Yale
Holmes Daniel, foreman r 5714 Dearborn
Holmes D. E. clerk r 6602 Perry av
Holmes E. C. carpenter r 6359 Yale
Holmes George, plumber bds. 6636 Sangamon
Holmes Henry, mason r 615, 57th
HOLMES H. H. mgr. of The Warner Glass Bending Co. 701, 63d
Holmes James, plumber bds. 6636 Sangamon

FRANK D. THOMASON, | PATENTS | 142 Dearborn Street.

APPENDIX TWO
A Holmes Chronology

1860
May 16
Herman Webster Mudgett is born at Gilmanton, New Hampshire.

1878
July 4
He is married to Clara A. Lovering at Alton, New Hampshire, by Justice of the Peace John W. Caurrier.

1887
January 28
He is married to Myrta Z. Belknap, under the name of Henry Howard Holmes.

February 14
He files in the Superior Court of Cook County, Illinois, a libel in divorce against his wife, Clara A. Lovering Mudgett, praying that their marriage may be dissolved.

1891
June 4
The said court orders this suit to be dismissed for default of appearance of complainant.

1893
March
He meets Miss Georgiana Yoke in Chicago.

September 19
He makes application for a twenty-year optional insurance policy for $10,000 in the Fidelity Mutual Life Association in which he avers: "Mother died at 58, don't remember the disease, no acute disease. Father died at 62 from injury to his foot."

November 9
Fidelity Mutual Life Association insures Benjamin F. Pitezel in the sum of $10,000.

Same month
Holmes is engaged to be married to Miss Yoke under the name of Henry Mansfield Howard.

1894

January 17
He is married to Miss Yoke in Denver, Colorado, by the Reverend Mr. Wilcox, and they journey on their honeymoon to Fort Worth, Texas.

January–April
Mudgett and Pitezel (the former under the name of D. T. Pratt and the latter under the name of Benton T. Lyman) are in Fort Worth, Texas, where they engage in building a store property on land formerly owned by Minnie Williams.

April
Pitezel leaves Fort Worth and goes to Chicago.

May
Mudgett and Miss Yoke leave Fort Worth and journey to Denver, Colorado.

May 21
They make their appearance in St. Louis.

June 1
About this date Holmes (Mudgett) and Pitezel go to Memphis, Tennessee. In this vicinity they first consider the location of the place where they propose to execute the insurance fraud.

June 8
Holmes and wife return to St. Louis.

June 15
Holmes purchases a drug store in St. Louis, Missouri, upon which he gives a mortgage under the name of Howard.

213

A HOLMES CHRONOLOGY

July 19
Holmes is arrested in St. Louis by the Merrill Drug Company and sent to prison under a charge of fraud and for selling mortgaged property. The man "Brown," to whom he sold it, is supposed to have been Pitezel. During his imprisonment in the St. Louis jail he meets Marion C. Hedgepeth.

July 28
He is released on bail.

July 29
He is rearrested and again committed to prison.

July 31
He is again released on bail furnished by Miss Yoke.

August 2
He is in New York and Philadelphia.

August 4
Miss Yoke (Mrs. Howard) leaves Lake Bluff, Illinois, where she was visiting, and journeys to Philadelphia.

August 5
Sunday—Holmes meets Miss Yoke at Broad Street Station, Philadelphia, and takes her to a boarding house at 1905 North Eleventh Street (Dr. Adella Alcorn's). He tells Miss Yoke he is selling a patent letter copier.

August 9
Holmes telegraphs $157.50 (the semiannual premium on the Pitezel policy) to the Chicago office of the Fidelity Mutual Life Association.

August 17
Pitezel, under the name of B. F. Perry, rents 1316 Callowhill Street and pays $10 on account of the rent to Walter W. Shedaker, agent.

August 17
Holmes and Pitezel purchase secondhand furniture from John F. Hughes, 1037 Buttonwood Street, and have it sent to 1316 Callowhill Street.

August 18
Pitezel calls at the furniture store alone and purchases a cot and some old matting.

August 22
Eugene Smith calls upon Pitezel and sees Holmes pass into the house and go upstairs.

214

August 22–September 1
Pitezel is seen in and about 1316 Callowhill Street by a large number of persons.

September 1
Evening—Pitezel calls upon Holmes at 1905 North Eleventh Street.

September 2
Holmes leaves 1905 North Eleventh Street at about 10:30 A.M. He returns about 4:00 P.M. He tells his wife (Miss Yoke) that the man who called the evening before was a messenger from the Pennsylvania Railroad Company, and that he can have an interview with a Pennsylvania Railroad official the next day at Nicetown. This Sunday morning he says he is going out to Nicetown to see the official, and that if he is successful, and as their week is up, they will probably start west that night.

September 2
Evening—Holmes and Miss Yoke leave Philadelphia on the 10:25 train and go direct to Indianapolis.

September 3
They arrive in Indianapolis and register at the Stubbins House.

September 4
They take boarding at 488 North Illinois Street, Indianapolis.

September 4
Pitezel's body is found at 1316 Callowhill Street by Eugene Smith.

September 5
Coroner holds first inquest.

September 6
Holmes goes to St. Louis, calls upon Mrs. Pitezel, and tells her to go to Howe with the papers, meaning insurance policy, etc. She takes papers to Howe. Holmes tells her that a body has been substituted for her husband and that "Ben is alive and all right," and not to worry.

September 8
Fidelity Mutual receives a telegraphic dispatch from George B. Stadden, manager for Missouri, at St. Louis, stating that "B. F. Perry, found dead in Philadelphia, is claimed to be B. F. Pitezel, who is insured on 044145. Investigate before remains leave there." About this time Howe writes to the company in Philadelphia, stating that he is counsel for Mrs. Pitezel, the beneficiary under the policy, and will come on with a member of the family to identify the body, etc.

215

September 13
Pitezel's body is buried as B. F. Perry in Potter's Field, Philadelphia.

September 5–19
Holmes is with Miss Yoke at her mother's home in Franklin, Indiana, leaving her, he says, to go to St. Louis again, or to Cincinnati, and then to Indianapolis. At this time Holmes is occasionally with his other wife at Wilmette, Illinois. He is likely with her on September 11. At Indianapolis he tells Miss Yoke that he has heard from the Pennsylvania Railroad official in Philadelphia about the copier and they are ready to pay over the money and have directed him to come on at once. He leaves her at the Circle Park Hotel, Indianapolis, and goes to Philadelphia.

September 17
He writes a letter to Mr. Cass, Chicago cashier of Fidelity Mutual, stating that his wife (in Wilmette) has told him that information is wanted of B. F. Pitezel, who was found in *Chicago* as B. F. Perry.

September 18
He writes another letter to Cass, saying that he overhears the body is in Philadelphia, *not in Chicago*, and that he will go to Philadelphia if his expenses are paid.

September 19
Holmes leaves Indianapolis for Philadelphia. He again stops at 1905 North Eleventh Street—Dr. Alcorn's.

September 20
He calls at the office of the company in Philadelphia, 914 Walnut Street. He tells Mr. Fouse, president of the company, that he has corresponded with Cass. He asks Fouse *about the circumstances of the death*, which Fouse relates briefly. Holmes says it is a very peculiar case and asks Mr. Fouse the cause of death, etc.

September 20
Alice writes her first letter to the home folks.

PHILADELPHIA, PA.
   Cor. Filbert & 11th sts., Sept. 20, 1894.
Dear Mamma and the rest:
   Just arrived in Philadelphia this morning and I wrote you yesterday of this. Mr. Howe and I have each a room at the above address. I am going to the Morgue after awhile. We stopped off at Washington, Md., this morning, and that made it six times that we transferred to different cars. Yesterday we got on the C. and O. Pullman car and it was crowded so I had to sit with some one Mr. Howe sit with some man we sit there quite awhile and pretty soon some one came

216

and shook hands with me. I looked up and here it was Mr. Howard. He did not know my jacket, but he said he thought it was his girl's face so he went to see and it was me. I don't like him to call me babe and child and dear and all such trash. When I got on the car Tuesday night Mr. Howe asked me if I had any money and I told him 5 cents so he gave me a dollar. How I wish I could see you all and hug the baby. I hope you are better. Mr. H. says that I will have a ride on the ocean. I wish you could see what I have seen. I have seen more scenery than I have seen since I was born I don't know what I saw before. This is all the paper I have so I will have to close & write again. You had better not write to me here for Mr. H. says that I may be off tomorrow. If you are worse wire me good-bye kisses to all and two big ones for you and babe. Love to all.

E. ALICE PITEZEL.

September 21

Howe and Alice Pitezel call at insurance office. Holmes calls same time. They meet as strangers, although they have traveled together from some point in Ohio to Washington, D.C. (Howe and Alice got off at Washington, and Holmes took train for Philadelphia. Howe and Alice came to Philadelphia on later train.) That day Holmes takes Alice out to see the sights of the city, and then to Dr. Alcorn's that night, stating that she (Alice) is his little sister. Alice sleeps in the third story next to Holmes' room, which opens to it. Alice has previously stopped with Howe at the Imperial Hotel, Eleventh and Filbert streets, from which place she wrote two letters. Following are copies:

Imperial Hotel
Eleventh, above Market Street,
Hendricks & Scott, Propr's.,
  PHILADELPHIA, PA., Sept. 21, 1894.
Dear Mamma and Babe:
  I have to write all the time to pass away the time.
  Mr. Howe has been away all morning. Mamma have you ever seen or tasted a red banana? I have had three. They are so big that I can just reach around it and have my thumb and next finger just tutch. I have not got any shoes yet and I have to go a hobbling around all the time. Have you gotten 4 letters from me besides this? Are you sick in bed yet or are you up? I wish that I could hear from you but I don't know whether I would get it or not. Mr. Howe telegraphed to Mr. Beckert and he said that he would write to you tonight. I have not got but two clean garments and that is a shirt and my white skirt. I saw some of the largest solid rocks that I bet you never saw. I crossed the Patomac River. I guess that I have told all the news; So good bye Kisses to you and babe,
  Yours loving daughter,

  MISS E. A. PITEZEL.
    If you are worse telegraph to the above address.
  Imperial Hotel,
  Eleventh above Market Street.

217

Imperial Hotel,
Eleventh above Market Street,
Hendricks & Scott, Propr's.,
  PHILADELPHIA,   189–.

Dear Dessa:

I thought I would write you a little letter and when I get to Mass. you must all write to me. Well this is a warm day here how is it there. Did you get your big washing done if I was there you would have a bigger one for I have a whole satchel full of dirty clothes. I bet that I have more fruit than all of you. Dessa I guess you are without shoes for I guess they don't intend to get me any. H. has come now so I guess I have to go to dinner.

Dessa take good care of mama. I will close your letter and write a little to Nell and Howard next time so good bye love to you with a kiss.

Dear Mama:

I was over to the insurance office this afternoon and Mr. Howe thinks there will be no trouble about getting it. They asked me almost a thousand questions, of course not quite so many. Is his nose broken or has he a Roman nose. I said it was broken. I will have to close and write more tomorrow so good bye love to all with kisses to all.

  Your loving daughter,
    E. ALICE PITEZEL.

September 21
At the conference at the company's office on this day, the marks of identification are agreed upon.

September 22
Pitezel's body is exhumed at Potter's Field. Holmes finds mole on neck and other marks of identification and says the body is that of B. F. Pitezel. Alice recognizes teeth of her father. He takes Alice to 1904 North Eleventh Street.

September 23
Holmes and Alice make affidavits before Coroner Ashbridge that the body found as B. F. Perry at 1316 Callowhill Street is that of Benjamin F. Pitezel. That evening Holmes and Alice leave for Indianapolis.

September 24
They arrive at Indianapolis. He registers Alice as "Etta Pitsel" in his handwriting.

September 24
Insurance company pays Howe $9,715.85, face of insurance policy, less expenses.

September 24
Alice writes another letter home. In these letters the allusion 4, 18, 8, is the children's cipher for Holmes.

Stubbins' European Hotel,
One square north of Union Depot on Illinois Street.
  INDIANAPOLIS, IND.,
    Sep. 24, 1894.
Dear Ones at Home:
  I am glad to hear that you are all well and that you are up. I guess you will not have any trouble in getting the money. 4, 18, 8 is going to get two of you and fetch you here with me and then I won't be so lonesome at the above address. I am not going to Miss Williams until I see where you are going to live and then see you all again because 4, 18, 8 is afraid that I will get two lonesome then he will send me on and go to school. I have a pair of shoes now if I could see you I would have a nough to talk to you all day but I cannot very well write it I will see you all before long though don't you worry. This is a cool day. Mr. Perry said that if you did not get the insurance all right through the lawyers to rite to Mr. Foust or Mr. Perry. I wish I had a silk dress. I have seen more since I have been away than I ever saw before in my life. I have another picture for your album. I will have to close for this time now so good bye love and kisses and squesses to all.
  Yours daughter,
    ETTA PITEZEL.
  P.O. I go by Etta here 4, 18, 8 told me to O Howard O Dessa, O Nell O Mamma, O Baby. Nell you & Howard will come with 4, 18, 8, & Mamma and Dessa later on won't you or as Mamma says.
    ETTA PITEZEL.

September 25
Holmes goes to St. Louis and remains there until the twenty-eighth.

September 27
Holmes gets $6,700 of the insurance money out of the $7,200 received by Mrs. Pitezel from Howe. He gives her the bogus note.

September 28
Holmes takes Nellie and Howard from Mrs. Pitezel at St. Louis. Alice joins them at Indianapolis, and she goes with Holmes, Nellie, and Howard to Cincinnati, where Holmes registers at the Atlantic House under the name of "Alexander E. Cook and three children."

September 29
He rents 305 Poplar Street from Mr. J. C. Thomas and takes a large stove to this

house. Overnight on the twenty-eighth he remains at Atlantic House, and on the twenty-ninth he takes them to Hotel Bristol, registers there as "A. E. Cook and three children," and remains there until Sunday, September 30, when he leaves with the children for Indianapolis and registers them at Hotel English as "Three Canning children."

October 1
Mrs. Pitezel leaves St. Louis for Galva, Illinois, with Dessie and the baby. Galva was the home of her parents. Holmes takes the children to the Circle House, Indianapolis (registers as "Three Canning children"), where they remain until October 10.

October 1
Alice and Nellie write letters, as follows:

INDIANAPOLIS, IND.,

October 1st., 1894.
Dear Mamma.

We was in Cincinnati yesterday and we got here last night getting that telegram from Mr. Howe yesterday afternoon.

Mr. H. is going to-night for you and he will take this letter. We went us three over to the Zoological Garden in Cincinnati yesterday afternoon and we saw all the different kinds of animals. We saw the ostrich it is about a head taller than I am so you know about how high it is. And the giraffe you have to look up in the sky to see it. I like it lots better here than in Cincinnati. It is such a dirty town Cin.

There is a monument right in front of the hotel where we are at and I should judge that it is about 3 times the hight of a five story building. I guess I have told all the news so good bye love to all & kisses. Hope you are all well.

Your loving daughter,
ETTA PITEZEL.

INDIANAPOLIS, IND.,
Oct. 1st, 1894.
Dear Mamma, Baby and D.

We are all well here. Mr. H. is going on a late train to-night. He is not here now I just saw him go by the Hotel He went some place I don't know where I think he went to get his ticket.

We are staying in another hotel in Indianapolis it is a pretty nice one we came here last night from C.

I like it lots better than in C. It is quite worm here and I have to wear this warm dress becaus my close an't ironet. We ate dinner over to the Stibbins Hotel where Alice staid and they knew her to. We are not staying there we are at the English H.

We have a room right in front of a monument and I think it was A. Lincolns.

Come as soon as you can because I want to see you and baby to. It is awful nice place where we are staying I don't think you would like it in Cincinnati either but Mr. H. sais he likes it there.

Good bye your dau.
NELLIE PITEZEL.

October 5
Holmes rents the house at Irvington from Mr. Crouse (J. C. Wand's clerk). He says he wants it for his sister, Mrs. A. E. Cook, and her children, and that she intends using it as a boardinghouse.

October 6
Nellie writes home:

INDIANAPOLIS, Ind.,
October 6, 1894.
Dear Mamma, Grandma and Grandpa:
We are all well here. It is a little warmer to-day. There is so many buggies go by that you cant hear yourself think. I first wrote you a letter with a crystal pen, but I made some mistakes and then I am in a hustle because Mr. H. has to go at 3 o'clock I don't know where. It is all glass so I hafto be careful or else it will break, it was only five cents. Mr. H. went to T. H. Indiana last night again. Their was a poor boy arrested yesterday for stealing a shirt he said he had no home the policeman said he would buy him a suit of clothes and then send him to a reform school. The patrols are lots different here than they are in St. Louis & Chicago. they couldnt get away if they wanted to. We hafto get up early if we get breakfast. We have awful good dinners pie fruit and sometimes cake at supper and this aint half. They are all men that eat at the tables we do not eat with them we have a room to ourselves. They are dutch but they can cook awful nice. Their is more bicycles go by her in one day than goes by in a month in St. Louis. I saw two great big ostriges alive and we felt of their feathers they are awful smooth 1/2 they are black with white tails they are as big as a horse. Why have buffaloes got big rings in their noses for I want Grandma and grandpa to write to me. Is the baby well and does he like coco I want you to all write why dont you write mama. I will close for this time goodby write

Yours truly,
NELLIE PITEZEL
over
Alices eyes hurts so she wont write this time.

October 7
Alice writes home today:

INDIANAPOLIS, IND.
Oct. 6th 1894.

Dear Mamma.
We are all well except I have got a bad cold and I have read so much in Uncle Tom's book that I could not see to write yesterday when Nell and Howard did. I am wearing my new (ders) dress today because it is warmer to day. Nell Howard and I have all got a crystal pen all made of glass five cents a piece and I am writing with it now. I expect Grandma and Grandpa was awful glad to see you. The hotel we are staying at faces right on a big wide bulvard and there is more safties and bugies passing than a little bit and how I wish I had a safty. Last Sunday we was at the Zoological Garden in Cincinnati, O. And I expect this Sunday will pass away slower than I dont know what and Howard is two dirty to be seen out on the street to-day. Why dont you write to me. I have not got a letter from you since I have been away and it will be three weeks day after tomorrow. It is raining out now quite hard. Nell is drawing now. The hotel is just a block from Washington Street and that is where all the big stores are. There is a shoe store there And there has been a man painting every day this week. They give these genuine oil painting away with every $1.00 purchas of shoes with small extra charge for frames. You cant get the pictures with out the frames though I wish I could get one you dont know how pretty they are. We go there every day and watch him paint. He can paint a picture in 1 1/2 minutes aint that quick. Nell keeps joring the stand so I can hardly write I mad half a dozen mistakes on the other side because she made me. This letter is for you all because I cant write to so many of you I guess I have told all the news so good bye love to all and kisses
Your loving daughter
E. ALICE PITEZEL
P.O. Write soon Howard got a box of collars and took one out and lost box and all the contents.

October 8
Alice writes another letter home:

Monday morning.
Do Mamma
Just got a letter from you saying that the babe was cross and Dessa and Grandma was sick. How is Grandpa I hope you will all feel better I thought you would not be home sick at all when you got there but it seems as though you are awful homesick Who met you at the depot did you get there Saterday or Sunday. I dont like to tell you but you ask me so I will have to. H. wont mind me at all He wanted a book and I got life of Gen. Sheridan and it is awful nice but now he dont read it at all hardly. One morning Mr. H. told me to tell him to stay in the next morning that he wanted him and he would come and get him and take him

out and I told him and he would not stay in at all he was out when he came. We have written two or three letters to you and I guess you will begin to get them now I will send this with my letter that I wrote yesterday and didnt send off Hope you will all keep well

         continued

    I have just finished Uncle Tom's Cabin and it is a nice book. I wish I could see you all. This is another cold day. We pay $12.00 a week for our room and board and I think that is pretty cheap for the good meals we have Yesterday we had mashed potatoes, grapes, chicken glass of milk each ice cream each a big sauce dish full awful good too lemon pie cake dont you think that is pretty good. They are Germans. I guess I will have to close so good bye, love to all and kisses. Write soon keep well

    Yours Truly

        E. ALICE PITEZEL.

October 10

Howard disappears on this day.

October 10

Holmes takes Alice and Nellie from the Circle House.

October 12

Evening—Holmes arrives in Detroit, he and Miss Yoke in one party, Alice and Nellie in another. He registers the children at the New Western Hotel as "Etta and Nellie Canning, St. Louis, Mo." He registers himself and Miss Yoke at the Hotel Normandie, "G. Howell and wife, Adrian."

October 13

Mrs. Pitezel, Dessie, and the baby leave Galva, Illinois, for Detroit, stopping in Chicago. Holmes has written to her that "Ben" is waiting to see her in Detroit.

October 13

Holmes and Miss Yoke remove from Hotel Normandie to 54 Park Place. He gives their names as "Mr. and Mrs. Holmes."

October 14

Mrs. Pitezel, Dessie, and the baby arrive in Detroit, and register as "C. A. Adams and daughter" at Geis' Hotel.

October 14

Alice writes her last letter:

    Detroit Michigan.

        October 14, 1894.

Dear Grandma and Grandpa,

    Hope you are all well Nell and I have both got colds and chapped hands but that is all. We have not had any nice weather at all I guess it is coming winter now. Tell mama that I have to have a coat. I nearly freeze in that thin jacket. We have to stay in all the time. Howard is not with us now. We are right near the Detroit River. We was going a boat riding yesterday but it was too cold. All that Nell and I can do is to draw and I get so tired siting that I could get up and fly almost. I wish I could see you all. I am geting so homesick that I don't know what to do. I suppose Wharton walks by this time don't he I would like to have him here he would pass away the time a goodeal.

October 15
Holmes takes Alice and Nellie to boardinghouse of Lucinda Burns, at 91 Congress Street.

October 15
About this date Holmes rents from Mr. Boninghausen the house at 241 East Forest Avenue. Mr. Boninghausen does not remember name Holmes gave. In the rear of cellar under porch of the house Holmes digs a hole four feet long, three and a half feet wide, three feet six inches deep.

October 18
Holmes and Miss Yoke leave Detroit for Toronto, Canada. He tells Mrs. Pitezel that Ben has gone to Toronto. At Toronto Holmes registers at Walker House as "Geo. H. Howell and wife, Columbus." Same day Mrs. Pitezel, Dessie, and the baby leave Geis' Hotel, Detroit, for Toronto; they are met at Grand Trunk Depot by Holmes and taken to the Union House, where they register under the name of "C. A. Adams and daughter."

October 19
Alice and Nellie leave Detroit for Toronto, arrive in the evening about eight o'clock, and are met by Holmes, who turns them over to George Dennis, a hotel porter for the Albion Hotel. They are registered as "Etta and Nellie Canning, Detroit."

October 20
Holmes rents house, 16 St. Vincent Street, from Mrs. Nudel. Says his name is Howard and that he wants it for his sister. Same day Holmes and Miss Yoke go to Niagara Falls.

October 21
They return and register at the Palmer House under the name of "Howell."

October 24
Holmes borrows a spade from Thomas W. Ryves, 18 St. Vincent Street, to dig a hole in the cellar "for the storage of potatoes." While in Toronto, Holmes calls at Albion Hotel for Alice and Nellie every morning, returning them in the evening.

October 25
On the morning of this day he takes Alice and Nellie from the Albion Hotel, paying their account for board in full. The children disappear.

October 25
He requests Mrs. Pitezel to go to Ogdensburg. He tells her Ben is in Montreal. He says that he has rented a house in Toronto, but that two detectives on bicycles are watching it, and it will not be safe for Ben to visit her there.

October 26
Holmes and Miss Yoke leave Toronto and go to Prescott, Canada, and remain there overnight.

October 31
He is found at Burlington, Vermont, at the Burlington House, registered as "G. D. Hale, Columbus, Ohio." He moves to rooms at Mr. Ahern's, where he gives the names of himself and Miss Yoke as "Mr. Hall and wife."

November 1
He rents a house, 26 Winooski Avenue, from W. B. McKillip, under the name of J. A. Judson, for his sister Mrs. Cook.

November 1–16
Between these dates he visits his parents at his old home in Gilmanton, New Hampshire, and resumes his relations with his real wife, Mrs. Mudgett. He tells a romantic story accounting for his absence from home.

November 17
He is arrested in Boston.

November 18
He makes his first confession. He says Pitezel is alive in South America, or on his way there, and that the children are with him. He says Pitezel was bound for San Salvador and that their means of communication was to be in the personal column of the New York *Herald*. Mrs. Pitezel is arrested on the same day.

November 20
Holmes and Mrs. Pitezel are brought to Philadelphia and committed to county prison.

December 6
Mrs. Pitezel makes a full statement to Mr. Fouse and Mr. Perry of the Fidelity Mutual Life Association.

December 15
Holmes now says Pitezel is dead and that the children were given to Miss Williams, who took them to Europe.

225

A HOLMES CHRONOLOGY

December 17
He makes another confession, declaring that Pitezel is dead and that he committed suicide.

1895

June 3
Holmes is tried for conspiracy to cheat and defraud the insurance company, and on the second day of the trial pleads guilty.

June 27
Detective Geyer leaves Philadelphia and commences his search for the children.

July 15
Geyer finds the bodies of Alice and Nellie in the cellar of the Toronto house, 16 St. Vincent Street.

July 20
Search begins of the Holmes "murder castle" in Chicago.

August 27
Geyer finds the remains of Howard in the house at Irvington, a few miles from Indianapolis.

September 12
Holmes is indicted in Philadelphia for the murder of Benjamin F. Pitezel.

September 23
He pleads not guilty. The court fixes the day of the trial to be October 28.

October 28
Motion for continuance is denied. Trial commences and continues until November 2. Jury renders a verdict: "Guilty of murder in the first degree."

November 18
Motion for a new trial is argued.

November 30
Motion for new trial is overruled. Holmes is sentenced to be hanged.

1896

May 7
Holmes is executed in the Philadelphia county prison.

226

INDEX

INDEX